Love in the Kitchen: A Valentine's Day Cookbook

Romantic Recipes and Tips for a Perfect Celebration

Love in the Kitchen: A Valentine's Day Cookbook

David Meyer

Published by DNT Publishing, 2024.

While every precaution has been taken in the preparation of this book, the publisher assumes no responsibility for errors or omissions, or for damages resulting from the use of the information contained herein.

LOVE IN THE KITCHEN: A VALENTINE'S DAY COOKBOOK

First edition. January 30, 2024.

Copyright © 2024 David Meyer.

ISBN: 979-8224835638

Written by David Meyer.

Table of Contents

Table of Contents

Introduction

Appetizers for Two

Soups for Lovebirds

Main Courses to Melt Hearts

Sides of Passion

Glossary

Introduction

Welcome to the Valentine's Day Cookbook, where love is not only celebrated but also savored through the art of delightful culinary experiences. In these pages, you'll discover a collection of recipes crafted to add a touch of romance to your Valentine's Day celebration. Whether you're a seasoned chef or just starting your culinary journey, these dishes are designed to be shared with someone special, creating moments that linger long after the last bite.

Why a Valentine's Day Cookbook?

Valentine's Day is a time to express love and affection, and what better way to do so than through the joy of cooking? This cookbook is more than just a collection of recipes; it's a guide to creating memorable, intimate meals that speak the language of the heart. Whether you're planning a romantic dinner for two, a cozy breakfast in bed, or a collaborative cooking experience with your significant other, you'll find inspiration within these pages.

Tips for a Romantic Culinary Experience

Before diving into the recipes, take a moment to explore our tips for creating the perfect romantic setting. From setting the table with care to selecting the right wine, we've included suggestions to elevate your dining experience. Cooking together can be a bonding adventure, and we've also provided ideas for couples' recipes to enhance the joy of preparing a meal as a team.

Welcome to the Valentine's Day Cookbook

Welcome to the Valentine's Day Cookbook, a culinary adventure designed to infuse romance and flavor into your celebration of love. Within these pages, you'll discover a curated selection of recipes tailored to create unforgettable moments with the one who holds the key to your heart.

Embark on a Culinary Journey of Love

Valentine's Day is a special occasion, and what better way to express your affection than through the art of cooking? Whether you're planning an intimate dinner, a cozy breakfast in bed, or a collaborative cooking experience, this cookbook is your guide to transforming ordinary meals into extraordinary expressions of love.

Crafted for Every Culinary Enthusiast

Whether you're a kitchen novice or a seasoned chef, the recipes in this cookbook are thoughtfully crafted to cater to all skill levels. Each dish is more than just a combination of ingredients – it's an invitation to savor the joy of creating something beautiful and delicious for someone special.

Elevate Your Celebration with Tips for Romance

To complement the delectable recipes, we've included tips for setting the perfect romantic ambiance. From table decor ideas to selecting the right wine, these suggestions aim to enhance the overall experience of your Valentine's Day celebration. Let the atmosphere, flavors, and shared moments intertwine to create a celebration that resonates with the essence of love.

Cooking Together, Creating Memories

In the spirit of togetherness, we've included recipes tailored for couples to enjoy cooking side by side. Strengthen your bond through shared laughter, culinary collaboration, and the joy of savoring a meal you've created together.

Tips for a Romantic Culinary Experience

Creating a romantic culinary experience goes beyond the ingredients and recipes; it's about crafting an atmosphere that enhances the connection between you and your loved one. Here are some tips to elevate your Valentine's Day celebration:

Set the Scene:

- Dim the lights and opt for candlelight to create a soft, romantic ambiance.

- Use elegant tableware, including your best dishes, glasses, and flatware.

- Consider decorating the table with fresh flowers, rose petals, or subtle romantic touches.

Select the Right Music:

- Create a playlist of your favorite romantic tunes or choose music that holds sentimental value.

- Opt for softer, instrumental melodies to enhance the intimate atmosphere.

Plan Thoughtful Details:

- Personalize the dining experience with handwritten notes or a heartfelt card.

- Consider incorporating elements that hold special meaning for both of you, such as a shared memory or an inside joke.

Choose an Intimate Setting:

- If weather permits, dine under the stars or set up a cozy indoor picnic with blankets and cushions.

- Select a location that allows for uninterrupted conversation and connection.

Pairing Wine with Love:

- Choose a wine that complements the meal and enhances the overall dining experience.

- Consider a wine-tasting experience where you both can explore and discuss different flavors.

Engage the Senses:

- Incorporate aromatic ingredients into your dishes to heighten the sensory experience.

- Experiment with textures and flavors to create a memorable and enjoyable meal.

Cook Together:

- Collaborative cooking can be a bonding experience. Choose recipes that involve both of you in the preparation process.

- Enjoy the journey of creating a meal together, and don't forget to taste-test along the way.

Capture the Moment:

- Take photos or create a scrapbook to commemorate your special Valentine's Day culinary adventure.

- Consider recording a video message for each other to revisit in the future.

Indulge in Dessert:

- Save room for a decadent dessert or create a dessert together as a sweet finale to your meal.

- Chocolate fondue, strawberries, or a special cake can add the perfect touch of sweetness.

Savor the Silence:

- Embrace moments of silence and enjoy the simple pleasure of each other's company.

- Let the flavors and aromas speak for themselves, allowing the meal to be a shared experience.

Appetizers for Two

Start your romantic culinary journey with enticing appetizers designed for sharing. These small bites are not only delicious but also set the perfect tone for a memorable Valentine's Day celebration.

Heart-shaped Caprese Skewers:

- Mini mozzarella balls, cherry tomatoes, and fresh basil leaves drizzled with balsamic glaze, artfully arranged on heart-shaped skewers.

Pomegranate and Goat Cheese Crostinis:

- Sliced baguette toasted to perfection, topped with creamy goat cheese, and garnished with pomegranate arils for a burst of flavor.

Romantic Roasted Red Pepper Hummus:

- Homemade hummus blended with roasted red peppers, garlic, and tahini, served with warm pita bread or crisp vegetable sticks.

Smoked Salmon and Cream Cheese Stuffed Cherry Tomatoes:

- Cherry tomatoes hollowed out and filled with a delightful mixture of smoked salmon and herbed cream cheese.

Strawberry Balsamic Bruschetta:

- Sliced strawberries, fresh basil, and balsamic glaze piled onto toasted baguette slices, creating a sweet and savory bruschetta.

Heart-shaped Caprese Skewers

These delightful and visually appealing heart-shaped caprese skewers are a perfect way to start your romantic meal. The classic combination of mozzarella, tomatoes, and basil gets a whimsical twist that is sure to capture your heart.

Ingredients:

- Fresh mozzarella balls (bocconcini)

- Cherry tomatoes

- Fresh basil leaves

- Balsamic glaze

- Olive oil

- Salt and pepper, to taste

- Heart-shaped skewers

Instructions:

Prepare the Ingredients:

- Drain the fresh mozzarella balls and set them aside.

- Wash the cherry tomatoes and pat them dry.

- Pick fresh basil leaves, ensuring they are clean and dry.

Assemble the Skewers:

- Take a heart-shaped skewer and slide on a cherry tomato, followed by a mozzarella ball, and then a basil leaf.

- Repeat the pattern, creating a heart shape on the skewer. Aim for 3-4 tomato-mozzarella pairs per skewer.

Drizzle with Balsamic Glaze:

- Arrange the assembled skewers on a serving platter.

- Drizzle the skewers with balsamic glaze, ensuring a light and even coating.

Season and Finish:

- Drizzle a touch of olive oil over the skewers for added richness.

- Sprinkle a pinch of salt and pepper to taste.

Serve with Love:

- Arrange the heart-shaped caprese skewers on a romantic serving plate.

- Present them with love and a flourish as the perfect start to your Valentine's Day celebration.

Pomegranate and Goat Cheese Crostinis

Elevate your Valentine's Day celebration with the exquisite blend of creamy goat cheese and vibrant pomegranate arils atop perfectly toasted baguette slices. These Pomegranate and Goat Cheese Crostinis are a symphony of flavors that will tantalize your taste buds.

Ingredients:

- Baguette, thinly sliced

- Goat cheese

- Pomegranate arils

- Honey, for drizzling

- Fresh thyme leaves (optional, for garnish)

Instructions:

Preheat the Oven:

- Preheat your oven to 375°F (190°C).

Slice and Toast the Baguette:

- Arrange the baguette slices on a baking sheet.

- Toast the slices in the preheated oven until they become golden and crispy. Keep an eye on them to prevent burning.

Spread Goat Cheese:

- Once the baguette slices are toasted, spread a generous layer of goat cheese on each slice while they are still warm.

Add Pomegranate Arils:

- Sprinkle a handful of pomegranate arils over the goat cheese, ensuring they are evenly distributed.

Drizzle with Honey:

- Drizzle honey over the crostinis for a touch of sweetness. The honey adds a delightful contrast to the tangy goat cheese and bursts of pomegranate flavor.

Garnish with Fresh Thyme (Optional):

- If desired, garnish each crostini with a few fresh thyme leaves for a herbal note.

Serve with Elegance:

- Arrange the Pomegranate and Goat Cheese Crostinis on a serving platter.

- Serve immediately, allowing your loved one to experience the delightful combination of textures and flavors.

Romantic Roasted Red Pepper Hummus

Add a touch of romance to your Valentine's Day celebration with this flavorful and velvety Roasted Red Pepper Hummus. The smoky sweetness of roasted red peppers combined with the creaminess of hummus creates a delightful dip that pairs perfectly with warm pita bread or crisp vegetable sticks.

Ingredients:

- 1 can (15 oz) chickpeas, drained and rinsed

- 2 large red bell peppers, roasted and peeled

- 3 tablespoons tahini

- 2 cloves garlic, minced

- 1/4 cup extra-virgin olive oil, plus extra for drizzling

- Juice of 1 lemon

- 1/2 teaspoon ground cumin

- Salt and pepper, to taste

- Pinch of cayenne pepper (optional, for a hint of spice)

- Fresh parsley, for garnish

Instructions:

Roast Red Peppers:

- Preheat your oven's broiler. Place whole red peppers on a baking sheet and broil, turning occasionally, until the skin is charred and blistered. Remove from the oven and place in a bowl covered with plastic wrap to steam. Once cooled, peel off the skin, remove seeds, and chop.

Prepare Chickpeas:

- In a food processor, combine chickpeas, roasted red peppers, tahini, minced garlic, lemon juice, cumin, salt, and pepper.

Blend Until Smooth:

● With the food processor running, gradually add olive oil until the hummus reaches a smooth and creamy consistency. Adjust seasoning to taste.

Add Optional Spice:

● For a subtle kick, add a pinch of cayenne pepper and blend again.

Serve in a Romantic Bowl:

● Transfer the Roasted Red Pepper Hummus to a romantic serving bowl.

Drizzle with Olive Oil and Garnish:

● Drizzle extra-virgin olive oil over the top and garnish with fresh parsley.

Pair and Enjoy:

● Serve the hummus with warm pita bread or an assortment of crisp vegetable sticks.

Savor the Romantic Flavor:

● Delight in the combination of smoky roasted red peppers and the creaminess of hummus, savoring each bite with your loved one.

Smoked Salmon and Cream Cheese Stuffed Cherry Tomatoes

Elevate your Valentine's Day appetizer with these elegant and flavorful Smoked Salmon and Cream Cheese Stuffed Cherry Tomatoes. The combination of creamy cheese, smoky salmon, and the burst of freshness from cherry tomatoes creates a bite-sized delight that's perfect for sharing.

Ingredients:

● Cherry tomatoes (about 20-24)

● Smoked salmon slices, thinly sliced

● Cream cheese softened

● Fresh dill, finely chopped

● Lemon zest

● Salt and pepper, to taste

● Capers, for garnish (optional)

Instructions:

Prepare Cherry Tomatoes:

- Cut a small slice off the bottom of each cherry tomato to create a flat base, allowing them to stand upright.

Hollow Out Tomatoes:

- Carefully scoop out the seeds and pulp from each cherry tomato using a small spoon or a melon baller, creating small tomato cups. Be gentle to avoid damaging the tomatoes.

Prepare Cream Cheese Mixture:

- In a bowl, combine softened cream cheese, finely chopped fresh dill, lemon zest, salt, and pepper. Mix until well combined.

Fill Tomatoes:

- Using a piping bag or a small spoon, fill each hollowed-out cherry tomato with the cream cheese mixture.

Add Smoked Salmon:

- Cut the smoked salmon slices into small pieces.

- Top each cream cheese-filled tomato with a piece of smoked salmon.

Garnish with Dill and Capers:

- Garnish each stuffed tomato with a sprinkle of fresh dill.

- Optionally, add capers for an extra burst of flavor and visual appeal.

Arrange and Serve:

- Arrange the Smoked Salmon and Cream Cheese Stuffed Cherry Tomatoes on a serving platter.

Chill and Serve:

- For the best flavor, chill the stuffed tomatoes in the refrigerator for a short time before serving.

Delight in Every Bite:

- Share these delightful and elegant bites with your loved one, savoring the perfect blend of creamy cheese, smoky salmon, and the freshness of cherry tomatoes.

Strawberry Balsamic Bruschetta

Indulge in the sweet and savory harmony of this Strawberry Balsamic Bruschetta – a delightful twist on the classic appetizer. The combination of ripe strawberries, fresh basil, and tangy balsamic glaze atop crisp baguette slices creates a burst of flavors that's perfect for a romantic start to your Valentine's Day celebration.

Ingredients:

- Fresh strawberries, diced

- Fresh basil leaves, chiffonade (thinly sliced)

- Balsamic glaze

- Baguette, thinly sliced

- Goat cheese (optional)

- Extra-virgin olive oil

- Honey, for drizzling

- Salt and black pepper, to taste

Instructions:

Preheat the Oven:

- Preheat your oven to 375°F (190°C).

Prepare Baguette Slices:

- Arrange the thinly sliced baguette on a baking sheet.

- Drizzle olive oil over each slice and toast in the preheated oven until golden and crispy.

Dice Strawberries:

- Dice fresh strawberries into small, bite-sized pieces.

Chiffonade Basil:

- Chiffonade the fresh basil leaves by stacking them, rolling them tightly, and slicing them thinly.

Assemble Strawberry Mixture:

- In a bowl, combine diced strawberries and basil. Drizzle balsamic glaze over the mixture and gently toss until well coated.

Spread Goat Cheese (Optional):

- If using goat cheese, spread a thin layer on each toasted baguette slice.

Top Baguette Slices:

- Spoon the strawberry and basil mixture onto each baguette slice.

Drizzle with Balsamic Glaze and Honey:

- Drizzle additional balsamic glaze over the top for extra flavor.

- Optionally, drizzle honey for a touch of sweetness.

Season and Serve:

- Sprinkle a pinch of salt and black pepper over the bruschetta.

- Arrange the Strawberry Balsamic Bruschetta on a serving platter.

Delight in the Fusion of Flavors:

- Share these delightful bites with your loved one, enjoying the fusion of sweet strawberries, aromatic basil, and tangy balsamic glaze.

Soups for Lovebirds

Warm your hearts and savor the intimate moments with these delectable Soups for Lovebirds. From creamy bisques to aromatic broths, these recipes are crafted to bring comfort and flavor to your romantic Valentine's Day dinner.

Creamy Tomato Basil Bisque:

- A velvety blend of ripe tomatoes, fragrant basil, and a touch of cream, creates a classic and comforting bisque.

Aphrodisiac Asparagus Soup:

- A light and elegant asparagus soup infused with delicate herbs, stimulating the senses for a romantic dining experience.

Spicy Shrimp and Avocado Gazpacho:

- A chilled gazpacho featuring succulent shrimp, creamy avocado, and a hint of spice, offers a refreshing and invigorating start to your meal.

Roasted Red Pepper and Tomato Love Potion Soup:

- A passionate soup with the smoky sweetness of roasted red peppers and the rich depth of tomatoes, blending into a love-infused potion.

Creamy Lobster Bisque:

- Indulge in the luxurious flavors of lobster and velvety cream, creating a soup that's both decadent and perfect for a special occasion.

Creamy Tomato Basil Bisque

Savor the classic comfort of a Creamy Tomato Basil Bisque, a velvety soup that blends the richness of tomatoes with the aromatic freshness of basil. This dish is perfect for a romantic evening, bringing warmth and flavor to your Valentine's Day celebration.

Ingredients:

- 2 tablespoons olive oil

- 1 onion, finely chopped

- 2 cloves garlic, minced

- 2 cans (28 oz each) whole peeled tomatoes

- 1 cup vegetable broth

- 1/2 cup heavy cream

- 1/4 cup fresh basil leaves, chopped

- Salt and pepper, to taste

- Pinch of sugar (optional, to balance acidity)

Instructions:

Sauté Aromatics:

- In a large pot, heat olive oil over medium heat. Add finely chopped onion and sauté until translucent. Add minced garlic and cook for an additional minute until fragrant.

Add Tomatoes:

- Pour in the cans of whole peeled tomatoes, breaking them apart with a spoon as they cook. Include the tomato juice from the cans.

Simmer:

- Add vegetable broth to the pot. Bring the mixture to a simmer and let it cook for about 15-20 minutes, allowing the flavors to meld.

Blend:

- Using an immersion blender or transferring to a regular blender in batches, blend the soup until smooth and creamy.

Add Cream and Basil:

● Return the soup to the pot and stir in the heavy cream. Add fresh basil leaves and let the soup simmer for an additional 5-10 minutes.

Season to Perfection:

● Season the Creamy Tomato Basil Bisque with salt and pepper to taste. If the tomatoes are too acidic, add a pinch of sugar to balance the flavors.

Serve with Love:

● Ladle the bisque into bowls and garnish with additional basil leaves. Optionally, drizzle a touch of olive oil on top.

Enjoy the Creamy Delight:

● Share this velvety delight with your loved one, savoring the comforting blend of tomatoes and basil that warms the soul.

Aphrodisiac Asparagus Soup

Ignite the senses with the delicate and alluring flavors of Aphrodisiac Asparagus Soup. Infused with the essence of asparagus and fragrant herbs, this light and elegant soup is crafted to enhance the romantic atmosphere of your Valentine's Day dinner.

Ingredients:

- 1 lb fresh asparagus, tough ends trimmed

- 1 onion, chopped

- 2 cloves garlic, minced

- 3 cups vegetable broth

- 1 potato, peeled and diced

- 1/2 cup heavy cream

- 2 tablespoons fresh chives, chopped

- 1 tablespoon fresh tarragon, chopped

- Salt and pepper, to taste

- Lemon zest, for garnish (optional)

Instructions:

Sauté Aromatics:

- In a large pot, sauté chopped onions in a bit of olive oil until softened. Add minced garlic and cook for an additional minute.

Add Asparagus and Potato:

- Cut the asparagus into 1-inch pieces. Add asparagus and diced potato to the pot, stirring to combine.

Pour in Vegetable Broth:

- Pour in the vegetable broth, ensuring the asparagus and potato are fully submerged. Bring the mixture to a gentle boil, then reduce the heat to a simmer.

Simmer Until Tender:

- Simmer the ingredients until the asparagus and potato are tender. This usually takes around 15-20 minutes.

Blend to Smooth Consistency:

● Using an immersion blender or transferring to a regular blender in batches, blend the soup until it reaches a smooth and creamy consistency.

Add Cream and Herbs:

● Stir in the heavy cream, fresh chives, and fresh tarragon. Allow the soup to simmer for an additional 5-7 minutes.

Season to Taste:

● Season the Aphrodisiac Asparagus Soup with salt and pepper to taste.

Serve with a Romantic Touch:

● Ladle the soup into bowls and garnish with additional fresh herbs. For a burst of freshness, add optional lemon zest.

Enjoy the Seductive Flavors:

● Share this tantalizing soup with your loved one, letting the delicate flavors of asparagus and herbs create a sensory experience.

Spicy Shrimp and Avocado Gazpacho

Refresh your palate and invigorate your senses with the tantalizing flavors of Spicy Shrimp and Avocado Gazpacho. This chilled soup, featuring succulent shrimp, creamy avocado, and a hint of spice, is a perfect start to your romantic Valentine's Day dinner.

Ingredients:

- 1 lb medium-sized shrimp, peeled and deveined

- 2 avocados, diced

- 4 large tomatoes, diced

- 1 cucumber, peeled and diced

- 1/2 red onion, finely chopped

- 3 cups tomato juice

- 1/4 cup fresh cilantro, chopped

- 1/4 cup fresh lime juice

- 2 cloves garlic, minced

- 1 jalapeño, seeded and minced (adjust to taste)

- Salt and black pepper, to taste

- Olive oil, for drizzling

- Fresh cilantro leaves, for garnish

Instructions:

Cook Shrimp:

> ● Bring a pot of salted water to a boil. Add shrimp and cook until they turn pink and opaque. Drain and set aside to cool.

Prepare Vegetables:

> ● In a large bowl, combine diced avocados, tomatoes, cucumber, and finely chopped red onion.

Chop Cilantro and Jalapeño:

> ● Chop fresh cilantro and jalapeño.

Assemble Gazpacho Base:

● Add the cooked shrimp to the bowl of vegetables. Pour in the tomato juice, fresh lime juice, minced garlic, chopped cilantro, and minced jalapeño. Mix well.

Chill the Gazpacho:

● Cover the bowl and refrigerate the gazpacho for at least 1-2 hours, allowing the flavors to meld.

Season to Taste:

● Before serving, season the gazpacho with salt and black pepper to taste. Adjust the spice level if needed.

Serve Chilled:

● Ladle the Spicy Shrimp and Avocado Gazpacho into bowls.

Drizzle with Olive Oil and Garnish:

● Drizzle a bit of olive oil over each bowl. Garnish with fresh cilantro leaves for a burst of color and flavor.

Enjoy the Chilled Spice:

● Share this refreshing and spicy gazpacho with your loved one, savoring the cool and invigorating flavors of shrimp and avocado.

Roasted Red Pepper and Tomato Love Potion Soup

Immerse yourselves in the rich and passionate flavors of the Roasted Red Pepper and Tomato Love Potion Soup. This captivating soup, featuring the smoky sweetness of roasted red peppers and the luscious depth of tomatoes, is a perfect addition to your romantic Valentine's Day dinner.

Ingredients:

- 3 large red bell peppers

- 6 ripe tomatoes, halved

- 1 onion, chopped

- 3 cloves garlic, minced

- 4 cups vegetable broth

- 1/4 cup tomato paste

- 2 tablespoons olive oil

- 1 teaspoon dried basil

- 1 teaspoon dried oregano

- Salt and pepper, to taste

- Fresh basil leaves, for garnish

Instructions:

Roast Red Peppers and Tomatoes:

- Preheat the oven broiler. Place red bell peppers and halved tomatoes on a baking sheet. Broil until the skin of the peppers is charred and the tomatoes are roasted. Remove from the oven and let them cool. Once cooled, peel and dice the peppers.

Sauté Aromatics:

- In a large pot, heat olive oil over medium heat. Add chopped onions and sauté until softened. Add minced garlic and cook for an additional minute.

Add Roasted Peppers and Tomatoes:

- Add the diced roasted red peppers and roasted tomatoes to the pot.

Blend Mixture:

- Using an immersion blender or transferring to a regular blender in batches, blend the mixture until smooth.

Create Tomato Base:

- In a bowl, mix the tomato paste with a bit of vegetable broth to create a smooth paste. Add this paste to the blended red pepper and tomato mixture.

Add Vegetable Broth and Seasonings:

- Pour in the remaining vegetable broth. Add dried basil, dried oregano, salt, and pepper. Stir well.

Simmer:

- Allow the soup to simmer for about 15-20 minutes, letting the flavors meld.

Adjust Seasoning:

- Taste and adjust the seasoning as needed. If the soup is too thick, you can add more vegetable broth.

Serve with Love:

- Ladle the Roasted Red Pepper and Tomato Love Potion Soup into bowls. Garnish with fresh basil leaves.

Enjoy the Love-Infused Soup:

- Share this aromatic and love-infused soup with your special someone, savoring the smoky sweetness of roasted red peppers and the luscious depth of tomatoes.

Creamy Lobster Bisque

Indulge in the luxurious and velvety texture of Creamy Lobster Bisque, a decadent soup that exudes elegance and flavor. Perfect for a special Valentine's Day dinner, this bisque combines the richness of lobster with a smooth creaminess that will leave you and your loved one enchanted.

Ingredients:

- 2 lobster tails (about 8 oz each), shells removed and meat chopped

- 1/4 cup unsalted butter

- 1 onion, finely chopped

- 2 carrots, peeled and diced

- 2 celery stalks, diced

- 3 cloves garlic, minced

- 1/4 cup all-purpose flour

- 1/4 cup tomato paste

- 1/2 cup brandy or dry sherry

- 4 cups seafood or fish broth

- 2 cups whole milk

- 1 cup heavy cream

- 1 bay leaf

- 1/2 teaspoon dried thyme

- Salt and pepper, to taste

- Chopped fresh parsley, for garnish

Instructions:

Sauté Vegetables:

> - In a large pot, melt butter over medium heat. Add finely chopped onion, diced carrots, diced celery, and minced garlic. Sauté until the vegetables are softened.

Add Lobster Meat:

> - Add the chopped lobster meat to the pot and sauté until the lobster turns opaque.

Stir in Flour and Tomato Paste:

- Sprinkle the flour over the lobster and vegetable mixture. Stir well to coat. Add tomato paste and continue stirring until well combined.

Deglaze with Brandy:

- Pour brandy or dry sherry into the pot to deglaze, scraping any flavorful bits from the bottom.

Pour in Broth, Milk, and Cream:

- Add seafood or fish broth, whole milk, and heavy cream to the pot. Stir well to combine.

Add Herbs and Seasoning:

- Toss in the bay leaf and dried thyme. Season with salt and pepper to taste. Stir and let the bisque simmer for about 15-20 minutes, allowing the flavors to meld.

Discard Bay Leaf:

- Remove the bay leaf from the pot.

Blend for Creamy Consistency:

- Using an immersion blender or transferring to a regular blender in batches, blend the bisque until it reaches a smooth and creamy consistency.

Adjust Seasoning:

- Taste and adjust the seasoning as needed.

Serve with Elegance:

- Ladle the Creamy Lobster Bisque into bowls. Garnish with chopped fresh parsley.

Savor the Decadence:

- Share this decadent bisque with your loved one, savoring the rich and luxurious flavors of lobster in a creamy embrace.

Main Courses to Melt Hearts

Ignite the flame of love with these enchanting main courses, designed to melt hearts and create a memorable Valentine's Day dining experience. From succulent meats to indulgent pasta dishes, these recipes are crafted to celebrate the essence of romance.

Filet Mignon with Red Wine Reduction:

- Tender filet mignon steaks cooked to perfection and drizzled with a rich red wine reduction. This classic dish is sure to impress with its melt-in-your-mouth goodness.

Lobster Linguine in Creamy Garlic Sauce:

- Luxurious lobster paired with al dente linguine, all bathed in a velvety creamy garlic sauce. This pasta dish is a delightful combination of elegance and indulgence.

Duck Breast with Cherry Port Wine Sauce:

- Pan-seared duck breasts with a luscious cherry port wine sauce. The sweet and savory flavors create a symphony of taste that's perfect for a romantic dinner.

Salmon En Papillote with Lemon and Dill:

- Salmon fillets delicately seasoned with lemon and dill, then wrapped in parchment paper and baked to perfection. This dish not only tantalizes the taste buds but also provides an elegant presentation.

Stuffed Bell Peppers with Quinoa and Shrimp:

- Colorful bell peppers stuffed with a delightful mixture of quinoa and shrimp, create a dish that's not only visually appealing but also bursting with flavor.

Chicken Marsala with Mushrooms:

- Succulent chicken breasts cooked in a Marsala wine sauce with earthy mushrooms. This classic Italian dish is both comforting and romantic.

Vegetarian Eggplant Parmesan:

- Layers of thinly sliced eggplant, marinara sauce, and melted mozzarella create a vegetarian delight that's hearty and satisfying.

Beef Wellington with Mushroom Duxelles:

- A show-stopping dish featuring beef tenderloin encased in flaky puff pastry and flavorful mushroom duxelles. This classic masterpiece is perfect for special occasions.

Shrimp Scampi with Linguine:

● Plump shrimp sautéed in a garlic and white wine sauce, then tossed with linguine. This dish is light, flavorful, and perfect for a romantic evening.

Veal Piccata with Lemon Caper Sauce:

● Tender veal cutlets pan-seared and served in a zesty lemon caper sauce. This dish is a burst of citrusy freshness that complements the delicate veal.

Lobster Linguine with Champagne Cream Sauce

Elevate your Valentine's Day dinner with the decadent and luxurious flavors of Lobster Linguine in Champagne Cream Sauce. This indulgent pasta dish combines succulent lobster with al dente linguine, all enveloped in a velvety champagne-infused cream sauce. Prepare to dazzle your loved one with this exquisite culinary creation.

Ingredients:

- 2 lobster tails, shells removed, and meat chopped

- 8 oz linguine pasta

- 1/2 cup unsalted butter

- 1 shallot, finely chopped

- 2 cloves garlic, minced

- 1 cup dry champagne

- 1 cup heavy cream

- Zest of 1 lemon

- Salt and black pepper, to taste

- Fresh parsley, chopped, for garnish

Instructions:

Cook Linguine:

- Cook the linguine pasta according to package instructions until al dente. Drain and set aside.

Sauté Lobster Tails:

- In a large skillet, melt 2 tablespoons of butter over medium heat. Add the chopped lobster tails and sauté until they are cooked through and opaque. Remove the lobster from the skillet and set aside.

Sauté Shallot and Garlic:

- In the same skillet, add the remaining butter. Sauté finely chopped shallot and minced garlic until softened and fragrant.

Deglaze with Champagne:

- Pour dry champagne into the skillet to deglaze, scraping any flavorful bits from the bottom of the pan.

Add Heavy Cream and Lemon Zest:

● Pour in the heavy cream and add lemon zest to the skillet. Stir well to combine.

Simmer Sauce:

● Let the sauce simmer for a few minutes until it thickens slightly. Season with salt and black pepper to taste.

Combine Lobster and Linguine:

● Add the sautéed lobster back into the skillet. Stir in the cooked linguine, ensuring it is well-coated with the champagne cream sauce.

Garnish and Serve:

● Garnish the Lobster Linguine with chopped fresh parsley. Serve immediately, allowing the flavors to shine.

Celebrate with Elegance:

● Share this elegant and indulgent dish with your loved one, savoring the exquisite combination of lobster, linguine, and champagne cream sauce.

Filet Mignon with Red Wine Reduction

Create a culinary masterpiece for your Valentine's Day celebration with this exquisite Filet Mignon dish featuring a rich Red Wine Reduction. Impress your loved one with the perfect combination of tender filet mignon and a velvety red wine sauce that adds depth and sophistication to your romantic dinner.

Ingredients:

- 2 filet mignon steaks (6-8 oz each)

- Salt and black pepper, to taste

- 2 tablespoons olive oil

- 1/2 cup red wine (choose a good-quality red wine)

- 1/2 cup beef broth

- 2 tablespoons unsalted butter

- 1 teaspoon Dijon mustard

- Fresh thyme or rosemary sprigs, for garnish

Instructions:

Season Filet Mignon:

- Season the filet mignon steaks generously with salt and black pepper on both sides. Let them come to room temperature for about 30 minutes.

Preheat Oven:

- Preheat your oven to 400°F (200°C).

Sear Filet Mignon:

- In an oven-safe skillet, heat olive oil over medium-high heat. Sear the filet mignon steaks for 2-3 minutes on each side until a golden crust forms.

Finish in the Oven:

- Transfer the skillet to the preheated oven and roast the filet mignon for about 5-7 minutes medium-rare or longer if you desire a different level of doneness.

Rest Filet Mignon:

- Remove the steaks from the oven and let them rest on a plate, covered with foil, for at least 5 minutes. This allows the juices to be redistributed.

Prepare Red Wine Reduction:

- In the same skillet over medium heat, add red wine and beef broth. Bring it to a simmer, scraping the browned bits from the bottom of the pan.

Add Butter and Mustard:

- Stir in unsalted butter and Dijon mustard. Continue simmering until the sauce thickens to your desired consistency.

Season and Strain Sauce:

- Season the red wine reduction with salt and black pepper to taste. Optionally, strain the sauce for a smoother texture.

Plate Filet Mignon:

- Place the rested filet mignon steaks on serving plates.

Pour Red Wine Reduction:

- Spoon the rich red wine reduction over the filet mignon steaks.

Garnish and Serve:

- Garnish with fresh thyme or rosemary sprigs for a touch of elegance.

Enjoy the Culinary Perfection:

- Share this perfectly cooked Filet Mignon with Red Wine Reduction with your loved one, savoring each bite of tender meat and flavorful sauce.

Lemon Herb Baked Salmon for Two

Create a light and flavorful Valentine's Day dinner with this delightful Lemon Herb Baked Salmon for Two. The combination of zesty lemon and aromatic herbs enhances the natural richness of salmon, making it a perfect choice for a romantic and healthy meal.

Ingredients:

- 2 salmon fillets (6-8 oz each)

- Salt and black pepper, to taste

- 2 tablespoons olive oil

- 2 tablespoons fresh lemon juice

- 2 cloves garlic, minced

- 1 teaspoon Dijon mustard

- 1 teaspoon fresh thyme leaves

- 1 teaspoon fresh rosemary, chopped

- Lemon slices, for garnish

- Fresh parsley, chopped, for garnish

Instructions:

Preheat Oven:

- Preheat your oven to 375°F (190°C).

Prepare Salmon Fillets:

- Pat the salmon fillets dry with paper towels. Season both sides with salt and black pepper.

Make Lemon Herb Marinade:

- In a bowl, whisk together olive oil, fresh lemon juice, minced garlic, Dijon mustard, fresh thyme leaves, and chopped rosemary.

Marinate Salmon:

- Place the salmon fillets in a shallow dish and pour the lemon herb marinade over them. Ensure the fillets are well-coated. Let them marinate for at least 15 minutes.

Bake Salmon:

● Transfer the marinated salmon fillets to a baking dish lined with parchment paper. Pour any remaining marinade over the top. Place lemon slices on each fillet.

Bake in the Oven:

● Bake the salmon in the preheated oven for approximately 15-20 minutes or until the salmon is cooked through and flakes easily with a fork.

Garnish and Serve:

● Remove the baked salmon from the oven and garnish with fresh chopped parsley. Serve the salmon fillets on individual plates.

Enjoy the Freshness:

● Share this Lemon Herb Baked Salmon with your loved one, savoring the fresh and vibrant flavors that make it a perfect choice for a romantic dinner.

Chicken Marsala with Mushrooms

Create a classic and romantic dinner with the rich and savory flavors of Chicken Marsala with Mushrooms. This timeless dish features tender chicken breasts in a Marsala wine sauce, accompanied by earthy mushrooms. Elevate your Valentine's Day celebration with this comforting and elegant recipe.

Ingredients:

- 2 boneless, skinless chicken breasts

- Salt and black pepper, to taste

- 1/2 cup all-purpose flour, for dredging

- 4 tablespoons unsalted butter

- 2 tablespoons olive oil

- 1 cup cremini or button mushrooms, sliced

- 1/2 cup Marsala wine

- 1/2 cup chicken broth

- 2 tablespoons fresh parsley, chopped, for garnish

Instructions:

Prepare Chicken Breasts:

- Season the chicken breasts with salt and black pepper. Dredge each chicken breast in flour, shaking off excess.

Sauté Chicken:

- In a large skillet, heat 2 tablespoons of butter and olive oil over medium-high heat. Sauté the chicken breasts until they are golden brown on both sides and cooked through. Remove the chicken from the skillet and set aside.

Sauté Mushrooms:

- In the same skillet, add the remaining butter. Sauté the sliced mushrooms until they are golden brown and tender.

Deglaze with Marsala Wine:

- Pour Marsala wine into the skillet, scraping the browned bits from the bottom. Let it simmer for a few minutes to reduce.

Add Chicken Broth:

- Pour in chicken broth and bring the mixture to a gentle simmer. Allow it to cook for an additional few minutes to melt the flavors.

Return Chicken to the Skillet:

- Return the cooked chicken breasts to the skillet, allowing them to warm up in the Marsala sauce. Cook for a few more minutes to let the chicken absorb the flavors.

Garnish and Serve:

- Garnish the Chicken Marsala with fresh chopped parsley. Serve the chicken breasts and mushrooms on individual plates.

Enjoy the Classic Dish:

- Share this Chicken Marsala with Mushrooms with your loved one, savoring the classic combination of tender chicken and the rich, Marsala wine-infused sauce.

Vegetarian Sweet Potato and Spinach Stuffed Portobello Mushrooms

Celebrate a delightful and flavorful Valentine's Day with these Vegetarian Sweet Potato and Spinach Stuffed Portobello Mushrooms. This meatless dish features a harmonious blend of sweet potatoes, spinach, and savory mushrooms, creating a wholesome and satisfying meal for you and your loved one.

Ingredients:

- 4 large Portobello mushrooms, stems removed

- 2 medium sweet potatoes, peeled and diced

- 2 cups fresh spinach, chopped

- 1 small onion, finely chopped

- 2 cloves garlic, minced

- 1/2 cup feta cheese, crumbled

- 1/4 cup pine nuts, toasted

- 2 tablespoons olive oil

- 1 teaspoon dried thyme

- Salt and black pepper, to taste

- Fresh parsley, chopped, for garnish

Instructions:

Preheat Oven:

- Preheat your oven to 375°F (190°C).

Prepare Portobello Mushrooms:

- Clean the Portobello mushrooms and remove the stems. Place them on a baking sheet.

Roast Mushrooms:

- Drizzle olive oil over the mushrooms and season with salt and black pepper—roast in the preheated oven for about 10 minutes to slightly soften.

Cook Sweet Potatoes:

- While the mushrooms are roasting, cook the diced sweet potatoes until they are tender. You can boil or steam them.

Sauté Spinach, Onion, and Garlic:

- In a skillet, heat olive oil over medium heat. Sauté chopped onion and minced garlic until softened. Add chopped spinach and cook until wilted.

Combine Sweet Potatoes and Spinach Mixture:

- In a bowl, combine the cooked sweet potatoes with the sautéed spinach mixture. Add dried thyme, crumbled feta cheese, and toasted pine nuts. Mix well.

Stuff Portobello Mushrooms:

- Stuff each Portobello mushroom with the sweet potato and spinach mixture, pressing it down gently.

Bake Stuffed Mushrooms:

- Return the stuffed Portobello mushrooms to the oven and bake for an additional 15-20 minutes or until the mushrooms are cooked through.

Garnish and Serve:

- Garnish the Vegetarian Sweet Potato and Spinach Stuffed Portobello Mushrooms with chopped fresh parsley. Serve them warm.

Enjoy the Wholesome Flavors:

- Share these flavorful and wholesome stuffed mushrooms with your loved one, savoring the combination of sweet potatoes, spinach, and savory mushrooms.

Sides of Passion

Complement your Valentine's Day dinner with these delightful and passion-infused side dishes, adding a touch of flavor and romance to your special meal.

Garlic Parmesan Roasted Asparagus:

- Tender asparagus spears roasted to perfection with garlic and Parmesan, creating a flavorful and elegant side dish.

Truffle Mashed Potatoes:

- Creamy mashed potatoes elevated with the luxurious essence of truffle oil, provide a decadent and indulgent side for your romantic dinner.

Balsamic Glazed Brussels Sprouts with Bacon:

- Brussels sprouts caramelized in a balsamic glaze and adorned with crispy bacon, offering a delightful balance of sweet and savory notes.

Honey Glazed Carrots with Thyme:

- Carrots glazed in sweet honey and thyme-infused coating, bring a burst of flavor and vibrant color to your dinner table.

Lemon Herb Quinoa Salad:

- A refreshing quinoa salad with a zesty lemon and herb dressing, providing a light and nutritious side dish.

Rosemary Garlic Roasted Potatoes:

- Baby potatoes roasted with aromatic rosemary and garlic, deliver a comforting and flavorful addition to your Valentine's Day feast.

Creamy Parmesan Risotto:

- Indulge in the creamy and velvety texture of Parmesan risotto, a classic side dish that pairs perfectly with a romantic dinner.

Cranberry Orange Pecan Salad:

- A vibrant salad featuring crisp mixed greens, dried cranberries, orange segments, and toasted pecans, drizzled with a citrus vinaigrette.

Grilled Zucchini with Lemon and Dill:

● Zucchini slices grilled to perfection and dressed with a bright lemon and dill seasoning, offering a light and flavorful side.

Wild Mushroom and Spinach Stuffed Tomatoes:

● Ripe tomatoes stuffed with a savory mixture of wild mushrooms and spinach, create an elegant and visually appealing side dish.

Garlic Parmesan Roasted Asparagus

Elevate your Valentine's Day dinner with the irresistible flavors of Garlic Parmesan Roasted Asparagus. This side dish combines the vibrant green goodness of asparagus with the rich and savory notes of garlic and Parmesan, creating a delightful and elegant addition to your romantic meal.

Ingredients:

- 1 bunch of asparagus, woody ends trimmed

- 2 tablespoons olive oil

- 3 cloves garlic, minced

- 1/4 cup grated Parmesan cheese

- Salt and black pepper, to taste

- Lemon wedges, for serving (optional)

- Fresh parsley, chopped, for garnish

Instructions:

Preheat Oven:

- Preheat your oven to 425°F (220°C).

Prepare Asparagus:

- Trim the woody ends of the asparagus spears. If the spears are thick, you can peel the bottom part for a more even texture.

Arrange on Baking Sheet:

- Place the trimmed asparagus on a baking sheet.

Drizzle with Olive Oil:

- Drizzle olive oil over the asparagus, ensuring they are evenly coated.

Sprinkle with Garlic and Parmesan:

- Sprinkle minced garlic and grated Parmesan cheese over the asparagus. Use your hands to toss the asparagus, making sure they are well-coated with the garlic and Parmesan.

Season with Salt and Pepper:

- Season the asparagus with salt and black pepper to taste.

Roast in the Oven:

- Roast the asparagus in the preheated oven for approximately 12-15 minutes or until they are tender and slightly crispy.

Garnish and Serve:

- Remove the roasted asparagus from the oven. Squeeze fresh lemon wedges over the top if desired. Garnish with chopped fresh parsley.

Enjoy the Garlicky Goodness:

- Share this Garlic Parmesan Roasted Asparagus with your loved one, savoring the garlicky goodness and the cheesy richness of this elegant side dish.

Truffle Mashed Potatoes

Add a touch of luxury to your Valentine's Day dinner with Truffle Mashed Potatoes. The earthy and aromatic essence of truffle oil elevates the classic mashed potatoes, creating a decadent and indulgent side dish that will impress your loved one.

Ingredients:

- 4 large russet potatoes, peeled and cut into chunks

- 1/2 cup unsalted butter

- 1/2 cup heavy cream

- 2 tablespoons truffle oil

- Salt and white pepper, to taste

- Fresh chives, chopped, for garnish

Instructions:

Boil Potatoes:

- Place the peeled and chopped potatoes in a large pot of salted water. Bring to a boil and simmer until the potatoes are fork-tender.

Drain and Mash:

- Drain the potatoes and mash them using a potato masher or ricer.

Heat Butter and Cream:

- In a small saucepan, heat the butter and heavy cream over low heat until the butter is melted.

Combine with Potatoes:

- Pour the warm butter and cream mixture over the mashed potatoes. Mix well until smooth and creamy.

Add Truffle Oil:

- Drizzle truffle oil over the mashed potatoes. Continue to mix until the truffle oil is evenly distributed.

Season with Salt and White Pepper:

- Season the truffle mashed potatoes with salt and white pepper to taste. Adjust the seasoning as needed.

Garnish with Chives:

● Garnish the mashed potatoes with chopped fresh chives for a burst of color and additional flavor.

Serve with Elegance:

● Share these Truffle Mashed Potatoes with your loved one, savoring the rich and indulgent combination of truffle and creamy potatoes.

Honey Glazed Carrots with Thyme

Add a touch of sweetness and herbaceous flavor to your Valentine's Day dinner with these Honey Glazed Carrots with Thyme. The natural sweetness of honey combined with the aromatic notes of thyme creates a delightful and vibrant side dish that complements your romantic meal.

Ingredients:

● 1 pound baby carrots, peeled

● 2 tablespoons unsalted butter

● 2 tablespoons honey

● 1 teaspoon fresh thyme leaves

● Salt and black pepper, to taste

● Fresh parsley, chopped, for garnish (optional)

Instructions:

Steam or Boil Carrots:

● Steam or boil the baby carrots until they are just tender. Drain and set aside.

Prepare Honey Glaze:

● In a skillet, melt the unsalted butter over medium heat. Add honey and fresh thyme leaves. Stir well to combine.

Glaze Carrots:

● Add the cooked baby carrots to the skillet with the honey-thyme glaze. Toss the carrots in the glaze, ensuring they are well-coated.

Season with Salt and Pepper:

● Season the honey-glazed carrots with salt and black pepper to taste. Adjust the seasoning as needed.

Simmer to Coat:

- Let the carrots simmer in the honey glaze for a few minutes, allowing them to absorb the flavors and become glossy.

Garnish and Serve:

- Remove the skillet from heat. Optionally, garnish the Honey Glazed Carrots with chopped fresh parsley for a burst of color.

Share the Sweetness:

- Share these Honey Glazed Carrots with Thyme with your loved one, savoring the perfect balance of sweetness and herbaceous goodness.

Balsamic Roasted Brussels Sprouts

Enhance your Valentine's Day dinner with the irresistible flavors of Balsamic Roasted Brussels Sprouts. The caramelized sweetness of balsamic glaze combined with the savory goodness of roasted Brussels sprouts creates a side dish that's both elegant and delicious.

Ingredients:

- 1 pound Brussels sprouts, trimmed and halved

- 2 tablespoons olive oil

- 2 tablespoons balsamic glaze

- Salt and black pepper, to taste

- 1/4 cup grated Parmesan cheese (optional)

- Toasted pine nuts, for garnish (optional)

Instructions:

Preheat Oven:

- Preheat your oven to 400°F (200°C).

Prepare Brussels Sprouts:

- Trim the ends of the Brussels sprouts and cut them in half.

Toss with Olive Oil and Balsamic Glaze:

- In a bowl, toss the halved Brussels sprouts with olive oil and balsamic glaze until they are evenly coated.

Season with Salt and Pepper:

● Season the Brussels sprouts with salt and black pepper to taste. Toss again to ensure even seasoning.

Roast in the Oven:

● Spread the Brussels sprouts in a single layer on a baking sheet. Roast in the preheated oven for about 20-25 minutes or until they are golden brown and crispy on the edges.

Optional Parmesan Cheese:

● If desired, sprinkle grated Parmesan cheese over the roasted Brussels sprouts during the last 5 minutes of roasting. This adds a cheesy richness to the dish.

Garnish with Pine Nuts:

● Optionally, garnish the Balsamic Roasted Brussels Sprouts with toasted pine nuts for an extra crunch.

Serve with Elegance:

● Arrange the roasted Brussels sprouts on a serving dish. Drizzle any remaining balsamic glaze from the baking sheet over the top.

Enjoy the Caramelized Goodness:

● Share these Balsamic Roasted Brussels Sprouts with your loved one, savoring the caramelized sweetness and crispy perfection of this elegant side dish.

Creamy Parmesan Risotto

Elevate your Valentine's Day dinner with the luxurious and velvety texture of Creamy Parmesan Risotto. This classic Italian dish, enriched with the nutty flavors of Parmesan cheese, creates a comforting and sophisticated side that perfectly complements your romantic meal.

Ingredients:

- 1 cup Arborio rice

- 1/2 cup dry white wine

- 4 cups chicken or vegetable broth, kept warm

- 1 small onion, finely chopped

- 2 tablespoons unsalted butter

- 2 tablespoons olive oil

- 1/2 cup grated Parmesan cheese

- Salt and black pepper, to taste

- Fresh parsley, chopped, for garnish

Instructions:

Sauté Onion:

- In a large pan or skillet, heat olive oil over medium heat. Add finely chopped onion and sauté until softened.

Toast Arborio Rice:

- Add Arborio rice to the pan and toast it for 1-2 minutes, stirring constantly until the edges become translucent.

Deglaze with White Wine:

- Pour in the dry white wine to deglaze the pan, stirring continuously until the wine is mostly absorbed by the rice.

Add Warm Broth:

- Begin adding the warm chicken or vegetable broth to the rice one ladle at a time. Allow the liquid to be absorbed before adding the next ladle. Stir frequently.

Continue Cooking:

● Continue adding broth and stirring until the rice is creamy and cooked to al dente texture. This process usually takes about 18-20 minutes.

Finish with Butter and Parmesan:

● Once the risotto reaches the desired consistency, stir in unsalted butter and grated Parmesan cheese. Mix until the butter and cheese are fully incorporated, creating a creamy texture.

Season and Garnish:

● Season the Creamy Parmesan Risotto with salt and black pepper to taste. Garnish with chopped fresh parsley for a burst of color and freshness.

Serve with Elegance:

● Spoon the risotto onto individual plates or a serving dish, ensuring a creamy and luxurious presentation.

Enjoy the Silky Perfection:

● Share this Creamy Parmesan Risotto with your loved one, savoring the silky perfection and rich flavors of this classic Italian dish.

Sweet Endings

Complete your romantic Valentine's Day dinner with these sweet and indulgent dessert options, providing the perfect finale for your memorable meal.

Chocolate-covered Strawberries:

- Juicy strawberries dipped in luscious dark or milk chocolate, create a decadent and romantic treat.

Molten Lava Cakes:

- Individual chocolate cakes with a gooey, molten center that oozes with rich chocolate goodness when cut open.

Red Velvet Cupcakes:

- Moist and velvety red velvet cupcakes topped with cream cheese frosting, offering a delightful balance of sweetness and tanginess.

Tiramisu:

- Layers of coffee-soaked ladyfingers and mascarpone cream, dusted with cocoa powder, create a classic and sophisticated Italian dessert.

Strawberry Shortcake:

- Fluffy shortcake biscuits layered with fresh strawberries and whipped cream, deliver a light and fruity sweetness.

Chocolate Mousse:

- Silky and airy chocolate mousse, served in elegant glasses or bowls, provides a heavenly ending to your romantic dinner.

Raspberry Chocolate Tart:

- A buttery tart crust filled with smooth chocolate ganache and adorned with fresh raspberries, creating a visually stunning and delicious dessert.

Vanilla Bean Panna Cotta:

- Creamy and velvety vanilla bean panna cotta served with a berry compote or caramel sauce for added flavor.

Pistachio and Raspberry Semifreddo:

● A semi-frozen Italian dessert with layers of pistachio and raspberry, offering a delightful combination of textures and flavors.

Decadent Chocolate Fondue:

● A communal dessert experience with a pot of warm, melted chocolate accompanied by an assortment of dippable treats like strawberries, marshmallows, and pretzels.

Decadent Chocolate Fondue

Create a memorable and interactive dessert experience with this Decadent Chocolate Fondue. Perfect for sharing, this warm and velvety chocolate fondue is accompanied by an array of dippable treats, making it an indulgent and romantic sweet ending to your Valentine's Day dinner.

Ingredients:

● 8 oz high-quality dark chocolate, chopped

● 1 cup heavy cream

● 2 tablespoons unsalted butter

● 1 teaspoon pure vanilla extract

● Assorted dippable's:

  ● Strawberries, washed and hulled

  ● Banana slices

  ● Marshmallows

  ● Pretzel sticks

  ● Cubes of pound cake

  ● Pineapple chunks

Instructions:

Prepare Dippables:

● Wash and prepare the assorted dippables, cutting fruits into bite-sized pieces and arranging them on a serving platter.

Chop Chocolate:

● Chop the high-quality dark chocolate into small pieces to facilitate even melting.

Make Chocolate Fondue:

- In a saucepan over medium heat, heat the heavy cream until it simmers but does not boil. Remove from heat and add the chopped chocolate, stirring continuously until the chocolate is fully melted and the mixture is smooth.

Add Butter and Vanilla:

- Stir in unsalted butter and pure vanilla extract until well combined. This enriches the chocolate fondue with a silky texture and added flavor.

Transfer to Fondue Pot:

- Transfer the chocolate fondue to a fondue pot or a heatproof bowl placed over a candle or fondue burner to keep it warm.

Dip and Enjoy:

- Dip the assorted treats into the warm chocolate fondue, coating them generously. Explore different combinations and savor the rich and velvety chocolate.

Create a Romantic Setting:

- Dim the lights, set out candles, and enjoy the intimate and romantic atmosphere as you indulge in the Decadent Chocolate Fondue with your loved one.

Celebrate Sweet Moments:

- Share this delightful and interactive dessert experience, creating sweet moments and memories together on Valentine's Day.

Raspberry Swirl Cheesecake Bars

Add a burst of fruity sweetness to your Valentine's Day dessert with these Raspberry Swirl Cheesecake Bars. The velvety cheesecake base is complemented by a vibrant raspberry swirl, creating a visually stunning and delicious treat for you and your loved one.

Ingredients:

For the Crust:

- 1 1/2 cups graham cracker crumbs

- 1/3 cup unsalted butter, melted

- 2 tablespoons granulated sugar

For the Cheesecake Filling:

- 16 oz cream cheese, softened

- 2/3 cup granulated sugar

- 2 large eggs

- 1 teaspoon vanilla extract

- 1/3 cup sour cream

For the Raspberry Swirl:

- 1 cup fresh or frozen raspberries

- 2 tablespoons granulated sugar

- 1 tablespoon water

- 1 teaspoon lemon juice

Instructions:

Preheat Oven:

- Preheat your oven to 325°F (163°C). Line a 9x9-inch baking pan with parchment paper, leaving an overhang on the sides for easy removal.

Prepare the Crust:

- In a bowl, combine graham cracker crumbs, melted butter, and granulated sugar. Press the mixture evenly into the bottom of the prepared baking pan.

Bake the Crust:

- Bake the crust in the preheated oven for 10 minutes. Remove from the oven and let it cool while you prepare the cheesecake filling.

Prepare Raspberry Swirl:

- In a saucepan, combine raspberries, granulated sugar, water, and lemon juice. Cook over medium heat, stirring occasionally, until the raspberries break down and the mixture thickens (about 5-7 minutes). Remove from heat and strain to remove seeds.

Make Cheesecake Filling:

- In a large bowl, beat the softened cream cheese until smooth. Add granulated sugar and beat until well combined. Add eggs one at a time, beating well after each addition. Stir in vanilla extract and sour cream until smooth.

Assemble Cheesecake Bars:

- Pour the cheesecake filling over the cooled crust. Drop spoonfuls of the raspberry swirl mixture on top. Use a skewer or knife to create a marbled effect by swirling the raspberry mixture into the cheesecake.

Bake Cheesecake Bars:

- Bake in the preheated oven for 35-40 minutes or until the edges are set and the center is slightly jiggly. The bars will continue to set as they cool.

Chill and Slice:

- Allow the Raspberry Swirl Cheesecake Bars to cool completely in the pan. Refrigerate for at least 4 hours or overnight. Once chilled, use the parchment overhang to lift the bars out of the pan and onto a cutting board. Cut into squares.

Serve and Enjoy:

- Serve these delightful Raspberry Swirl Cheesecake Bars as a sweet and romantic treat for your Valentine's Day celebration.

Strawberry Champagne Sorbet

Celebrate the sweetness of love with this elegant and refreshing Strawberry Champagne Sorbet. Combining the flavors of ripe strawberries and bubbly champagne, this sorbet is a delightful treat for a romantic Valentine's Day.

Ingredients:

- 2 cups fresh strawberries, hulled and halved

- 1 cup granulated sugar

- 1 cup champagne or sparkling wine

- 1 tablespoon lemon juice

- Zest one lemon

- Fresh mint leaves, for garnish (optional)

Instructions:

Prepare Strawberries:

- Wash, hull, and halve the fresh strawberries.

Make Simple Syrup:

- In a small saucepan, combine granulated sugar and 1 cup of water. Bring to a simmer over medium heat, stirring until the sugar dissolves completely. Allow the simple syrup to cool.

Blend Strawberries:

- In a blender, combine the halved strawberries, champagne, lemon juice, and lemon zest. Blend until smooth.

Strain Mixture:

- Strain the strawberry mixture through a fine-mesh sieve into a bowl to remove seeds and pulp.

Combine with Simple Syrup:

- Mix the strained strawberry puree with the cooled simple syrup. Stir well to combine.

Chill Mixture:

- Refrigerate the mixture for at least 2-3 hours or until it is thoroughly chilled.

Churn in Ice Cream Maker:

- Pour the chilled strawberry mixture into an ice cream maker and churn according to the manufacturer's instructions.

Freeze:

- Transfer the churned sorbet into a lidded container and freeze for an additional 2-4 hours or until firm.

Serve with Elegance:

- Scoop the Strawberry Champagne Sorbet into serving bowls or glasses. Garnish with fresh mint leaves if desired.

Toast to Love:

- Share this refreshing and romantic Strawberry Champagne Sorbet with your loved one, toasting the sweetness of your love on Valentine's Day.

Red Velvet Molten Lava Cakes

Indulge in the rich and velvety goodness of Red Velvet Molten Lava Cakes for a decadent and romantic Valentine's Day dessert. These individual cakes have a gooey molten center that flows out when cut, creating a delightful surprise for you and your loved one.

Ingredients:

- 1/2 cup unsalted butter

- 4 oz semi-sweet chocolate, chopped

- 1 cup powdered sugar

- 2 large eggs

- 2 egg yolks

- 1 teaspoon vanilla extract

- 1/4 cup all-purpose flour

- 2 tablespoons red velvet cake mix

- Pinch of salt

- Powdered sugar, for dusting (optional)

- Fresh berries, for garnish (optional)

Instructions:

Preheat Oven:

- Preheat your oven to 425°F (218°C). Grease and lightly flour four ramekins.

Melt Chocolate and Butter:

- In a heatproof bowl, melt the butter and chopped semi-sweet chocolate together. You can use a double boiler or microwave in short intervals, stirring until smooth.

Add Powdered Sugar:

- Stir in the powdered sugar until well combined.

Mix in Eggs and Vanilla:

- Add the eggs and egg yolks, one at a time, stirring well after each addition. Stir in the vanilla extract.

Incorporate Dry Ingredients:

- Gently fold in the all-purpose flour, red velvet cake mix, and a pinch of salt until just combined. Be careful not to overmix.

Fill Ramekins:

- Divide the batter evenly among the prepared ramekins.

Bake:

- Place the ramekins on a baking sheet and bake in the preheated oven for about 12-14 minutes. The edges should be set, but the center should still be soft.

Serve Immediately:

- Carefully run a knife around the edges of each cake and invert onto serving plates. The molten center should flow out.

Dust with Powdered Sugar and Garnish:

- Dust the Red Velvet Molten Lava Cakes with powdered sugar if desired. Garnish with fresh berries for a pop of color.

Enjoy the Decadence:

- Share these Red Velvet Molten Lava Cakes with your loved one, savoring the decadent and gooey center that makes each bite a delightful experience.

Dark Chocolate Covered Strawberries

Elevate the romance of Valentine's Day with the luscious combination of juicy strawberries and rich dark chocolate. These Dark Chocolate Covered Strawberries are an elegant and indulgent treat that is simple to make yet perfect for sharing with your loved one.

Ingredients:

- Fresh strawberries, washed and dried

- 8 ounces dark chocolate, finely chopped

- 1 tablespoon coconut oil (optional, for smoother chocolate)

- White chocolate for drizzling (optional)

- Chopped nuts, shredded coconut, or sprinkles for decoration (optional)

Instructions:

Prepare Strawberries:

- Ensure that the strawberries are completely dry. Line a baking sheet with parchment paper.

Melt Dark Chocolate:

- In a heatproof bowl, melt the dark chocolate. You can use a double boiler or microwave in short intervals, stirring until smooth. If desired, add coconut oil to achieve a smoother consistency.

Dip Strawberries:

- Holding each strawberry by the stem, dip it into the melted dark chocolate, allowing excess chocolate to drip off.

Place on Parchment Paper:

- Place the dipped strawberries on the parchment-lined baking sheet. Ensure they are not touching each other.

Optional Decoration:

- If you'd like to add decorations, sprinkle chopped nuts, shredded coconut, or sprinkles onto the chocolate-covered strawberries while the chocolate is still wet.

Drizzle with White Chocolate (Optional):

- If desired, melt white chocolate and drizzle it over the dark chocolate-covered strawberries for an elegant finish.

Chill:

- Place the baking sheet in the refrigerator for about 30 minutes to allow the chocolate to set.

Serve and Enjoy:

- Once the chocolate is fully set, arrange the Dark Chocolate Covered Strawberries on a serving plate. Share and enjoy this sweet and romantic treat with your loved one.

Romantic Toasting Drinks

Raise your glasses and toast to love with these romantic and delightful drinks. Whether you prefer a classic champagne toast or a unique cocktail, these beverages are perfect for celebrating the special moments of Valentine's Day.

Classic Champagne Toast:

- Pour chilled champagne or sparkling wine into elegant flutes. The effervescence and elegance of champagne make it a timeless choice for toasting to love.

Strawberry Bellini:

- Blend fresh strawberries and strain the puree. Pour the strawberry puree into champagne flutes and top with prosecco for a fruity and bubbly toast.

Pomegranate Mimosa:

- Combine pomegranate juice with champagne to create a vibrant and refreshing mimosa. Garnish with pomegranate arils for an extra touch.

Raspberry Rose Fizz:

- Muddle fresh raspberries at the bottom of a glass, add a splash of rose water, and top with sparkling water or prosecco for a fragrant and romantic drink.

Passionfruit Martini:

- Mix passionfruit juice, vodka, and a splash of simple syrup. Shake with ice and strain into martini glasses for a tropical and enticing cocktail.

Love Potion No. 9:

- Combine cranberry juice, raspberry liqueur, and vodka in a shaker with ice. Shake well and strain into glasses for a vibrant and flavorful love potion.

Chocolate-Covered Strawberry Martini:

- Mix chocolate liqueur, strawberry vodka, and cream in a shaker with ice. Strain into martini glasses and garnish with a chocolate-covered strawberry for a decadent treat.

Cranberry Champagne Cocktail:

- Pour cranberry juice and a splash of orange liqueur into champagne flutes. Top with champagne and garnish with a twist of orange peel for a zesty and bubbly concoction.

Lavender Lemonade Sparkler:

● Make lavender-infused simple syrup and mix it with freshly squeezed lemon juice. Top with sparkling water for a refreshing and aromatic drink.

Vanilla Chai White Russian:

● Combine vanilla vodka, chai tea concentrate, and cream over ice for a cozy and indulgent twist on the classic White Russian.

Love Potion Martini

Create a magical and enchanting atmosphere with the Love Potion Martini—a delightful and romantic cocktail that captures the essence of love. This pink-hued martini is both visually stunning and delicious, making it the perfect drink for toasting your special moments on Valentine's Day.

Ingredients:

- 2 oz raspberry vodka

- 1 oz elderflower liqueur

- 1 oz cranberry juice

- 1/2 oz fresh lemon juice

- 1/2 oz simple syrup

- Ice

- Fresh raspberries or edible flowers for garnish

Instructions:

Prepare Glassware:

- Chill your martini glasses in the freezer for at least 10 minutes before preparing the Love Potion Martinis.

Combine Ingredients:

- In a cocktail shaker, add raspberry vodka, elderflower liqueur, cranberry juice, fresh lemon juice, and simple syrup.

Add Ice:

- Fill the shaker with ice to the top.

Shake Well:

- Secure the lid on the shaker and shake vigorously for about 15-20 seconds. This chills the ingredients and creates a nice froth.

Strain into Glasses:

- Strain the Love Potion Martini mixture into the chilled martini glasses.

Garnish:

- Garnish each martini with fresh raspberries or edible flowers for an extra touch of romance.

Toast to Love:

• Raise your Love Potion Martinis and toast to the magic of love. Sip and savor the delightful flavors of this enchanting cocktail.

Sparkling Raspberry Lemonade

Quench your thirst with a refreshing and fizzy Sparkling Raspberry Lemonade. This vibrant beverage combines the tartness of fresh lemons with the sweetness of ripe raspberries, creating a delightful drink that's perfect for toasting on Valentine's Day.

Ingredients:

• 1 cup fresh raspberries

• 1 cup fresh lemon juice (about 6-8 lemons)

• 1/2 cup granulated sugar (adjust to taste)

• 4 cups cold sparkling water

• Ice cubes

• Lemon slices and fresh raspberries for garnish

• Mint leaves for garnish (optional)

Instructions:

Prepare Simple Raspberry Syrup:

• In a small saucepan, combine fresh raspberries and granulated sugar. Heat over medium heat, mashing the raspberries with a fork. Simmer for 5-7 minutes until the sugar is dissolved and the raspberries have released their juices.

Strain Raspberry Syrup:

• Strain the raspberry mixture through a fine-mesh sieve into a bowl, pressing to extract as much liquid as possible. Discard the solids and let the raspberry syrup cool.

Mix Lemonade:

• In a large pitcher, combine fresh lemon juice and the prepared raspberry syrup. Stir well to combine.

Add Sparkling Water:

• Just before serving, pour cold sparkling water into the pitcher. Stir gently to mix the lemonade and sparkling water.

Serve Over Ice:

- Fill glasses with ice cubes and pour the Sparkling Raspberry Lemonade over the ice.

Garnish:

- Garnish each glass with lemon slices, fresh raspberries, and mint leaves for a burst of color and freshness.

Toast and Enjoy:

- Raise your glasses filled with Sparkling Raspberry Lemonade and toast to the sweetness of love and special moments on Valentine's Day.

Red Velvet Hot Chocolate

Indulge in the cozy and decadent flavors of Red Velvet Hot Chocolate for a delightful treat on Valentine's Day. This rich and velvety hot chocolate, inspired by the classic red velvet cake, is sure to warm your heart and create a romantic atmosphere.

Ingredients:

- 4 cups whole milk

- 1/2 cup granulated sugar

- 1/4 cup unsweetened cocoa powder

- 1 teaspoon vanilla extract

- Red food coloring (as desired)

- Pinch of salt

- 4 ounces white chocolate, chopped

- Whipped cream for topping

- Red velvet cake crumbs for garnish (optional)

Instructions:

Prepare Hot Chocolate Base:

- In a saucepan over medium heat, combine whole milk, granulated sugar, unsweetened cocoa powder, vanilla extract, and a pinch of salt. Whisk the mixture until it is well combined and heated through.

Add Red Food Coloring:

- Add red food coloring to achieve the desired red velvet hue. Adjust the amount according to your preference.

Melt White Chocolate:

- Stir in the chopped white chocolate until it is fully melted and the hot chocolate becomes velvety and smooth.

Simmer (Optional):

- Allow the Red Velvet Hot Chocolate to simmer for a few minutes, stirring occasionally, to enhance the flavors.

Serve:

- Pour the red velvet hot chocolate into mugs.

Top with Whipped Cream:

- Add a generous dollop of whipped cream on top of each mug. The contrast of the red hot chocolate and the white whipped cream adds to the visual appeal.

Garnish (Optional):

- If desired, garnish with red velvet cake crumbs for an extra touch of indulgence.

Sip and Enjoy:

- Sip and savor the rich and comforting flavors of Red Velvet Hot Chocolate with your loved one, letting it warm your hearts on a cozy Valentine's Day.

Passionfruit Bellini

Elevate your Valentine's Day celebration with the exotic and fruity flavors of a Passionfruit Bellini. This sparkling cocktail is a delightful twist on the classic Bellini, adding a touch of passionfruit sweetness to your romantic toast.

Ingredients:

- 2 ripe passionfruits

- 1 tablespoon simple syrup (adjust to taste)

- Prosecco or champagne chilled

- Fresh mint leaves for garnish (optional)

Instructions:

Prepare Passionfruit Puree:

- Cut the passionfruits in half and scoop out the pulp into a bowl. Mash the pulp with a fork to create passionfruit puree.

Strain Seeds (Optional):

- If you prefer a smoother texture, strain the passionfruit puree through a fine-mesh sieve to remove the seeds.

Add Simple Syrup:

- Stir in simple syrup to the passionfruit puree, adjusting the sweetness to your liking.

Assemble Bellini:

- Spoon a tablespoon or more of the passionfruit puree into the bottom of each champagne flute.

Pour Prosecco:

- Top the passionfruit puree with chilled prosecco or champagne, filling the glass to your desired level.

Garnish (Optional):

- Garnish the Passionfruit Bellini with fresh mint leaves for a burst of color and fragrance.

Stir Gently:

- Give the Bellini a gentle stir to mix the passionfruit puree with the sparkling wine.

Toast to Love:

- Raise your glasses filled with Passionfruit Bellini and toast to the passion and love shared on Valentine's Day.

Cupid's Strawberry Mint Sparkler

Add a touch of romance to your Valentine's Day with Cupid's Strawberry Mint Sparkler—a refreshing and flavorful mocktail that combines the sweetness of strawberries with the invigorating essence of mint. This non-alcoholic beverage is perfect for toasting to love and creating a special moment.

Ingredients:

- 1 cup fresh strawberries, hulled and sliced

- 1 tablespoon granulated sugar

- 10-12 fresh mint leaves

- 1 tablespoon fresh lime juice

- 2 cups sparkling water or club soda, chilled

- Ice cubes

- Strawberry slices and mint sprigs for garnish

Instructions:

Prepare Strawberry Mint Mixture:

- In a bowl, combine sliced strawberries and granulated sugar. Allow the strawberries to macerate for about 10 minutes, releasing their juices.

Muddle Mint:

- In a separate glass, muddle fresh mint leaves to release their aromatic flavors.

Combine Strawberry Mint Mixture:

- Transfer the macerated strawberries along with their juices into a blender. Add the muddled mint leaves and fresh lime juice. Blend until you have a smooth strawberry-mint mixture.

Strain (Optional):

- If you prefer a smoother texture, strain the strawberry mint mixture through a fine-mesh sieve to remove any pulp.

Assemble the Sparkler:

- Fill glasses with ice cubes. Pour the strawberry mint mixture evenly among the glasses.

Top with Sparkling Water:

● Pour chilled sparkling water or club soda into each glass, filling to the top.

Garnish:

● Garnish the Cupid's Strawberry Mint Sparklers with additional strawberry slices and mint sprigs for a delightful presentation.

Stir Gently:

● Give the drink a gentle stir to combine the flavors.

Toast and Enjoy:

● Raise your glasses, toast to love, and enjoy the refreshing and romantic flavors of Cupid's Strawberry Mint Sparkler.

Romantic Breakfast-in-Bed Ideas

Surprise your loved one with a romantic breakfast in bed to start Valentine's Day on a special note. These ideas are not only delicious but also designed to create a cozy and intimate atmosphere.

Heart-Shaped Pancakes:

- Prepare a stack of heart-shaped pancakes using a heart-shaped mold. Serve with a drizzle of maple syrup, fresh berries, and a dusting of powdered sugar.

Eggs Benedict with Smoked Salmon:

- Create a classic Eggs Benedict with a romantic twist by adding smoked salmon. Top with a creamy hollandaise sauce and chives.

Avocado Rose Toast:

- Arrange slices of avocado in the shape of a rose on toasted artisan bread. Sprinkle with salt, pepper, and a dash of red pepper flakes.

Yogurt Parfait with Berries:

- Layer Greek yogurt with granola and a variety of fresh berries in a beautiful glass. Top with a drizzle of honey for sweetness.

Croissant French Toast:

- Dip croissants in a mixture of eggs, milk, and cinnamon, then cook them on a griddle until golden brown. Serve with whipped cream and berries.

Fruit and Cheese Board:

- Arrange a selection of fresh fruits, cheeses, and nuts on a wooden board. Add some honey or jam for a sweet touch.

Smoked Salmon Bagel with Cream Cheese:

- Spread cream cheese on a toasted bagel and top with smoked salmon, capers, red onion slices, and a sprinkle of dill.

Chia Seed Pudding Parfait:

- Layer chia seed pudding with fresh fruit and granola in a glass. Allow it to set overnight for a quick and healthy breakfast.

Heart-Shaped Waffles:

- Make heart-shaped waffles and serve with a dollop of whipped cream, strawberries, and a drizzle of chocolate or berry sauce.

Caprese Omelette:

- Prepare an omelet with cherry tomatoes, fresh mozzarella, and basil. Fold it into a heart shape for a romantic touch.

Cinnamon Roll Bake:

- Create a cozy atmosphere with the aroma of a cinnamon roll bake. Serve warm with a cream cheese glaze.

Chocolate Covered Strawberry Smoothie Bowl:

- Blend frozen strawberries, bananas, and cocoa powder for a chocolate-covered strawberry smoothie bowl. Top with sliced strawberries and dark chocolate shavings.

Heart-shaped Pancakes with Berries

Start your Valentine's Day with a sweet and romantic breakfast by serving heart-shaped pancakes with a delightful assortment of fresh berries. This simple yet charming dish is sure to make your loved one feel cherished.

Ingredients:

For the Pancakes:

- 1 cup all-purpose flour

- 2 tablespoons granulated sugar

- 1 teaspoon baking powder

- 1/2 teaspoon baking soda

- 1/4 teaspoon salt

- 3/4 cup buttermilk

- 1 large egg

- 2 tablespoons unsalted butter, melted

- 1 teaspoon vanilla extract

For Serving:

- Fresh strawberries, hulled and sliced

- Fresh blueberries

- Maple syrup

- Powdered sugar for dusting (optional)

Instructions:

Preheat Griddle or Pan:

- Preheat a griddle or non-stick pan over medium heat.

Prepare Dry Ingredients:

- In a mixing bowl, whisk together the flour, sugar, baking powder, baking soda, and salt.

Combine Wet Ingredients:

- In another bowl, whisk together the buttermilk, egg, melted butter, and vanilla extract.

Combine Wet and Dry Ingredients:

● Pour the wet ingredients into the dry ingredients and gently stir until just combined. Do not overmix; a few lumps are okay.

Shape Heart Pancakes:

● Grease the griddle or pan with a little butter or cooking spray. Pour small amounts of batter onto the griddle, shaping each pancake into a heart shape using a spoon.

Cook Until Bubbles Form:

● Cook the pancakes until bubbles form on the surface, then flip and cook the other side until golden brown.

Repeat:

● Repeat the process until all the batter is used, adjusting the heat as needed.

Serve:

● Stack the heart-shaped pancakes on a plate.

Add Fresh Berries:

● Top the pancakes with a generous amount of fresh strawberries and blueberries.

Drizzle with Maple Syrup:

● Drizzle maple syrup over the pancakes and berries.

Optional Dusting:

● Optionally, dust the pancakes with powdered sugar for an extra touch of sweetness.

Serve Warm:

● Serve the heart-shaped pancakes with berries warm and enjoy this delightful and romantic breakfast together.

Eggs Benedict with Smoked Salmon

Elevate your Valentine's Day breakfast with a luxurious twist on the classic Eggs Benedict. This recipe features perfectly poached eggs, smoked salmon, and a luscious hollandaise sauce—all served on a toasted English muffin. It's a delightful and indulgent way to start the day.

Ingredients:

For the Hollandaise Sauce:

- 3 large egg yolks

- 1 tablespoon lemon juice

- 1/2 cup unsalted butter, melted

- Pinch of cayenne pepper

- Salt to taste

For the Eggs Benedict:

- 4 large eggs

- 4 slices of smoked salmon

- 2 English muffins, split and toasted

- Fresh dill for garnish (optional)

- Salt and black pepper to taste

Instructions:

Prepare Hollandaise Sauce:

- In a blender or food processor, combine egg yolks and lemon juice. Blend until smooth.

Emulsify with Butter:

- With the blender running, slowly pour in the melted butter in a thin stream until the sauce thickens and emulsifies. Add cayenne pepper and salt to taste. Keep the hollandaise sauce warm.

Poach Eggs:

- Poach the eggs by bringing a pot of water to a gentle simmer. Add a splash of vinegar. Crack each egg into a small bowl and gently slide them into the simmering water. Poach for about 3-4 minutes for a runny yolk.

Assemble Eggs Benedict:

- Place the toasted English muffin halves on a plate. Top each half with a slice of smoked salmon.

Add Poached Eggs:

- Carefully place a poached egg on each slice of smoked salmon.

Drizzle with Hollandaise:

- Generously drizzle hollandaise sauce over the poached eggs.

Season and Garnish:

- Season with salt and black pepper to taste. Garnish with fresh dill if desired.

Serve Warm:

- Serve the Eggs Benedict with Smoked Salmon immediately while warm.

Optional Presentation:

- For a romantic touch, shape the hollandaise sauce into a heart or add a heart-shaped garnish.

Cinnamon French Toast Sticks

Transform your Valentine's Day breakfast into a delightful and shareable treat with these Cinnamon French Toast Sticks. Golden brown and coated in cinnamon sugar, these sticks are perfect for dipping into maple syrup or your favorite fruit compote.

Ingredients:

- 8 slices of thick-cut bread (white or brioche)

- 3 large eggs

- 1/2 cup milk

- 1 teaspoon vanilla extract

- 1/2 teaspoon ground cinnamon

- Pinch of salt

- 1/4 cup granulated sugar

- 1 teaspoon ground cinnamon (for coating)

- Butter or cooking spray for griddling

- Maple syrup for dipping

Instructions:

Cut Bread into Sticks:

- Trim the crusts off each slice of bread and cut it into sticks, creating the desired size for your French toast sticks.

Prepare Batter:

- In a shallow bowl, whisk together eggs, milk, vanilla extract, ground cinnamon, and a pinch of salt.

Dip Bread Sticks:

- Dip each breadstick into the egg mixture, ensuring it is well-coated on all sides.

Coat with Cinnamon Sugar:

- In a separate bowl, mix granulated sugar and ground cinnamon. Roll each dipped bread stick in the cinnamon sugar mixture until coated.

Preheat Griddle or Pan:

● Preheat a griddle or non-stick pan over medium heat. Add butter or cooking spray.

Cook French Toast Sticks:

● Place the coated bread sticks on the griddle or pan. Cook until golden brown on all sides, turning occasionally to ensure even cooking.

Serve Warm:

● Once the French toast sticks are golden and crisp, remove them from the griddle or pan.

Optional Heart Shape (if desired):

● For a romantic touch, use a heart-shaped cookie cutter to create heart-shaped French toast sticks.

Serve with Syrup:

● Arrange the Cinnamon French Toast Sticks on a plate and serve warm with maple syrup for dipping.

Enjoy Together:

● Share these delicious and cinnamon-sweet French toast sticks with your loved one for a special and cozy Valentine's Day breakfast.

Romantic Omelette with Goat Cheese and Herbs

Create a decadent and romantic breakfast with this exquisite Goat Cheese and Herbs Omelette. Filled with creamy goat cheese and fresh herbs, this omelet is a delightful way to start Valentine's Day.

Ingredients:

- 3 large eggs

- 2 tablespoons milk or cream

- Salt and black pepper to taste

- 2 tablespoons unsalted butter

- 2 ounces goat cheese, crumbled

- 1 tablespoon fresh chives, chopped

- 1 tablespoon fresh parsley, chopped

- 1 tablespoon fresh dill, chopped

- Extra herbs for garnish (optional)

Instructions:

Whisk Eggs:

- In a bowl, whisk together the eggs, milk or cream, salt, and black pepper until well combined.

Prepare Fresh Herbs:

- Chop the fresh chives, parsley, and dill.

Heat Butter:

- In a non-stick skillet, heat the butter over medium heat until melted and foamy.

Pour Egg Mixture:

- Pour the whisked egg mixture into the skillet.

Swirl and Cook:

- Swirl the skillet to spread the eggs evenly. Allow the eggs to set slightly around the edges.

Add Goat Cheese and Herbs:

● Sprinkle crumbled goat cheese evenly over one-half of the omelet. Add chopped chives, parsley, and dill on top of the goat cheese.

Fold and Cook:

● Carefully fold the other half of the omelet over the cheese and herbs using a spatula. Allow it to cook for an additional minute until the cheese melts.

Serve Warm:

● Slide the Goat Cheese and Herbs Omelette onto a plate and serve it warm.

Garnish (Optional):

● Garnish the omelet with extra fresh herbs for an added burst of flavor and a visually appealing touch.

Enjoy Together:

● Share this romantic omelet with your loved one, savoring the creamy goat cheese and the aromatic blend of fresh herbs.

Overnight Raspberry Almond Chia Pudding

Begin your Valentine's Day with a delightful and nutritious Overnight Raspberry Almond Chia Pudding. This make-ahead breakfast not only offers a burst of flavor from fresh raspberries but also provides a boost of energy to start the day on a healthy note.

Ingredients:

- 1/4 cup chia seeds

- 1 cup almond milk (or any milk of your choice)

- 1-2 tablespoons maple syrup or honey (adjust to taste)

- 1/2 teaspoon almond extract

- 1/2 cup fresh raspberries

- Sliced almonds for topping

- Fresh mint leaves for garnish (optional)

Instructions:

Mix Chia Seeds and Liquid:

- In a bowl or jar, combine chia seeds, almond milk, maple syrup or honey, and almond extract. Stir well to ensure the chia seeds are evenly distributed.

Add Raspberries:

- Gently fold in fresh raspberries into the chia seed mixture. Mash a few raspberries with a fork to release their juices for added flavor.

Cover and Refrigerate:

- Cover the bowl or jar and refrigerate the mixture overnight or for at least 4 hours. This allows the chia seeds to absorb the liquid and create a pudding-like consistency.

Stir Before Serving:

- Before serving, give the chia pudding a good stir to break up any clumps and ensure a smooth texture.

Top with Almonds:

- Sprinkle sliced almonds on top of the chia pudding for a crunchy element and added nuttiness.

Garnish (Optional):

● Garnish with fresh mint leaves for a touch of freshness and visual appeal.

Serve Chilled:

● Serve the Overnight Raspberry Almond Chia Pudding chilled.

Enjoy Together:

● Share this nutritious and delicious chia pudding with your loved one for a wholesome and delightful start to Valentine's Day.

Cooking Together: Couples' Recipes

Cooking together can be a fun and romantic activity for couples. Here's a set of recipes that are not only delicious but also designed for teamwork in the kitchen. Enjoy creating these dishes together and savor the moments of togetherness.

Appetizer: Heart-shaped Caprese Skewers

- A light and refreshing starter featuring heart-shaped mozzarella and tomato skewers drizzled with balsamic glaze.

Appetizer: Pomegranate and Goat Cheese Crostinis

- Crispy crostinis topped with creamy goat cheese and sweet pomegranate arils for a burst of flavor.

Appetizer: Romantic Roasted Red Pepper Hummus

- A smooth and flavorful roasted red pepper hummus, perfect for dipping with pita bread or vegetable sticks.

Appetizer: Smoked Salmon and Cream Cheese Stuffed Cherry Tomatoes

- Cherry tomatoes filled with a savory mixture of smoked salmon and cream cheese for a bite-sized treat.

Appetizer: Strawberry Balsamic Bruschetta

- Sliced strawberries mixed with balsamic glaze and basil on toasted baguette slices for a sweet and tangy bruschetta.

Soup: Creamy Tomato Basil Bisque

- A comforting and velvety tomato basil soup that's perfect for sharing.

Soup: Aphrodisiac Asparagus Soup

- A light and nutritious asparagus soup with a touch of aphrodisiac ingredients.

Soup: Spicy Shrimp and Avocado Gazpacho

- A refreshing and spicy cold soup with shrimp and avocado for a tropical twist.

Soup: Roasted Red Pepper and Tomato Love Potion Soup

- A vibrant soup with roasted red peppers and tomatoes, creating a love potion for your taste buds.

Main Course: Lobster Linguine with Champagne Cream Sauce

- Luxurious lobster paired with linguine and a decadent champagne cream sauce for a special main course.

Main Course: Filet Mignon with Red Wine Reduction

- Juicy filet mignon cooked to perfection and served with a rich red wine reduction sauce.

Main Course: Lemon Herb Baked Salmon for Two

- Baked salmon fillets infused with zesty lemon and aromatic herbs for a light and flavorful dish.

Main Course: Chicken Marsala with Mushrooms

- Tender chicken breasts cooked in a Marsala wine sauce with mushrooms for a classic and savory dish.

Main Course: Vegetarian Sweet Potato and Spinach Stuffed Portobello Mushrooms

- Portobello mushrooms stuffed with a flavorful mixture of sweet potatoes and spinach, perfect for a vegetarian option.

Sides: Garlic Parmesan Roasted Asparagus

- Asparagus spears roasted with garlic and Parmesan for a simple and tasty side dish.

Sides: Truffle Mashed Potatoes

- Creamy mashed potatoes elevated with the earthy flavor of truffle oil.

Sides: Honey Glazed Carrots with Thyme

- Carrots glazed with honey and infused with thyme for a sweet and aromatic side.

Sides: Balsamic Roasted Brussels Sprouts

- Brussels sprouts roasted with balsamic glaze for a caramelized and flavorful side dish.

Sides: Creamy Parmesan Risotto

- A classic and creamy Parmesan risotto that pairs well with any main course.

Dessert: Decadent Chocolate Fondue

- Melted chocolate served with an assortment of fruits and treats for dipping.

Dessert: Raspberry Swirl Cheesecake Bars

- Creamy cheesecake bars with a swirl of raspberry for a sweet and tangy finish.

Dessert: Strawberry Champagne Sorbet

- A refreshing and fruity sorbet with the effervescence of champagne.

Dessert: Red Velvet Molten Lava Cakes

- Individual red velvet lava cakes with a gooey, molten center.

Dessert: Dark Chocolate Covered Strawberries

- Classic and indulgent dark chocolate-covered strawberries for a romantic treat.

Drinks: Romantic Toasting Drinks

- Choose from a selection of romantic drinks to toast your special moments.

DIY Heart-shaped Pizza

Get creative and share a fun and personalized meal with your loved one by making your heart-shaped pizza. This DIY pizza activity adds a playful touch to your Valentine's Day celebration. Here's a simple recipe for crafting your heart-shaped masterpiece:

Ingredients:

For the Pizza Dough:

- 2 1/4 teaspoons active dry yeast

- 1 teaspoon sugar

- 1 cup warm water (110°F/43°C)

- 3 cups all-purpose flour

- 1 tablespoon olive oil

- 1 teaspoon salt

For the Pizza Toppings:

- 1 cup pizza sauce

- 2 cups shredded mozzarella cheese

- Your favorite pizza toppings (e.g., pepperoni, sliced bell peppers, olives, mushrooms)

Instructions:

Prepare Pizza Dough:

- In a small bowl, combine active dry yeast, sugar, and warm water. Let it sit for about 5 minutes until it becomes foamy.

Mix Dry Ingredients:

- In a large mixing bowl, combine flour and salt. Make a well in the center.

Combine Dough Ingredients:

- Pour the yeast mixture and olive oil into the well. Gradually incorporate the flour into the wet ingredients until a dough forms.

Knead Dough:

- Transfer the dough to a floured surface and knead for about 5-7 minutes until it becomes smooth and elastic.

Let Dough Rise:

- Place the dough in a lightly oiled bowl, cover it with a damp cloth, and let it rise in a warm place for 1-2 hours or until it doubles in size.

Preheat Oven:

- Preheat your oven to 475°F (245°C). If you have a pizza stone, place it in the oven during preheating.

Shape Heart:

- After the dough has risen, punch it down and transfer it to a floured surface. Divide the dough in half. Take one half and shape it into a heart by forming a round bottom and pinching the top to create a point.

Add Sauce and Toppings:

- Spread pizza sauce evenly over the heart-shaped dough, leaving a border around the edges. Sprinkle shredded mozzarella cheese and add your favorite toppings.

Bake:

- If using a pizza stone, transfer the pizza to the preheated stone. If not, place the pizza on a baking sheet. Bake in the preheated oven for 12-15 minutes or until the crust is golden and the cheese is bubbly and melted.

Repeat for the Second Heart:

- Repeat the process for the second half of the dough.

Serve Warm:

- Once baked, remove the heart-shaped pizzas from the oven and let them cool for a few minutes before slicing.

Enjoy Together:

- Share your DIY heart-shaped pizzas and enjoy a delicious and personalized meal with your loved one.

His and Hers Pasta Night

Create a special and personalized pasta night for you and your loved one with customized his or hers pasta dishes. Choose flavors and ingredients that cater to each other's preferences for a delightful and romantic dinner. Here are two unique pasta recipes:

For Him: Spicy Sausage and Mushroom Linguine

Ingredients:

- 8 oz linguine pasta

- 2 tablespoons olive oil

- 1/2 lb spicy Italian sausage, casings removed

- 1 cup cremini mushrooms, sliced

- 3 cloves garlic, minced

- 1/2 teaspoon red pepper flakes (adjust to taste)

- 1/2 cup chicken broth

- 1/2 cup heavy cream

- Salt and black pepper to taste

- Fresh parsley for garnish

- Grated Parmesan cheese for serving

Instructions:

Cook linguine pasta according to package instructions. Drain and set aside.

In a large skillet, heat olive oil over medium heat. Add the spicy Italian sausage, breaking it apart with a spatula as it cooks.

Once the sausage is browned, add sliced mushrooms and minced garlic to the skillet. Cook until mushrooms are tender.

Sprinkle red pepper flakes over the sausage and mushroom mixture for a spicy kick.

Pour in chicken broth and heavy cream, stirring to combine. Simmer for a few minutes until the sauce thickens.

Season with salt and black pepper to taste.

Toss the cooked linguine into the spicy sausage and mushroom sauce, ensuring the pasta is well coated.

Serve the Spicy Sausage and Mushroom Linguine garnished with fresh parsley and grated Parmesan cheese.

For Her: Creamy Shrimp and Spinach Fettuccine

Ingredients:

- 8 oz fettuccine pasta

- 2 tablespoons butter

- 1 lb large shrimp, peeled and deveined

- 3 cloves garlic, minced

- 1 cup cherry tomatoes, halved

- 2 cups fresh baby spinach

- 1 cup heavy cream

- Zest of 1 lemon

- Salt and black pepper to taste

- Fresh basil leaves for garnish

- Grated Parmesan cheese for serving

Instructions:

Cook fettuccine pasta according to package instructions. Drain and set aside.

In a large skillet, melt butter over medium heat. Add shrimp and cook until pink and opaque.

Add minced garlic to the skillet and sauté for a minute until fragrant.

Stir in halved cherry tomatoes and cook until they start to soften.

Add fresh baby spinach to the skillet, tossing until wilted.

Pour in heavy cream and lemon zest, stirring to combine. Simmer for a few minutes until the sauce thickens.

Season with salt and black pepper to taste.

Toss the cooked fettuccine into the creamy shrimp and spinach sauce, ensuring the pasta is well coated.

Serve the Creamy Shrimp and Spinach Fettuccine garnished with fresh basil leaves and grated Parmesan cheese.

Couples' Cooking Challenge

Turn your date night into an exciting and collaborative experience with a Couples' Cooking Challenge. Choose a set of mystery ingredients or specific themes for each course, and challenge yourselves to create unique dishes together. Here's a sample challenge with an appetizer, main course, and dessert:

Challenge Theme: Mediterranean Delights

Appetizer: Mediterranean Bruschetta Duo

Ingredients:

- Baguette slices

- Cherry tomatoes

- Feta cheese

- Kalamata olives

- Fresh basil leaves

- Olive oil

- Balsamic glaze

Challenge: Create two variations of Mediterranean-inspired bruschetta using the given ingredients.

Main Course: Greek-inspired Stuffed Peppers

Ingredients:

- Bell peppers (red, yellow, or green)

- Ground lamb or beef

- Rice

- Feta cheese

- Red onion

- Garlic

- Diced tomatoes

- Fresh parsley

- Lemon

- Greek seasoning (oregano, thyme, rosemary)

Challenge: Prepare stuffed peppers with a Greek twist using the provided ingredients.

Dessert: Honey Yogurt Parfait with Fresh Berries

Ingredients:

- Greek yogurt

- Honey

- Granola

- Fresh berries (strawberries, blueberries, raspberries)

- Mint leaves

Challenge: Create a visually appealing and delicious honey yogurt parfait using the listed ingredients.

Instructions:

Discuss the Challenge:

- Agree on the challenge theme and review the mystery ingredients for each course.

Divide Responsibilities:

- Assign tasks for each course. Decide who will take the lead on each dish.

Set a Time Limit:

- Challenge yourselves with a time limit for each course. This adds an element of excitement and encourages teamwork.

Get Creative:

- Encourage creativity and out-of-the-box thinking. Think about unique presentations and flavor combinations.

Cook Together:

- Work together in the kitchen, communicate, and enjoy the process of creating your dishes.

Presentation Matters:

- Pay attention to the presentation of your dishes. Arrange them on the plate in an aesthetically pleasing way.

Taste and Evaluate:

- Once the dishes are prepared, sit down, taste each other's creations, and evaluate them based on taste, presentation, and creativity.

Share the Experience:

- Reflect on the Couples' Cooking Challenge experience. Share laughs, successes, and even the challenges you faced during the cooking process.

Enjoy the Results:

- Sit back, relax, and enjoy the delightful Mediterranean-inspired meal you both created together.

Tiramisu for Two

Indulge in a romantic and classic Italian dessert with this Tiramisu for Two recipes. This individual serving of Tiramisu is perfect for sharing on a special occasion, such as Valentine's Day.

Ingredients:

- 2/3 cup strong brewed coffee, cooled

- 2 tablespoons coffee liqueur (e.g., Kahlúa), optional

- 2 large egg yolks

- 1/4 cup granulated sugar

- 1/2 cup mascarpone cheese, softened

- 1/2 cup heavy cream

- 1/2 teaspoon vanilla extract

- Ladyfinger cookies (enough to create two layers in serving glasses)

- Cocoa powder for dusting

- Chocolate shavings for garnish (optional)

Instructions:

Brew Coffee:

- Brew a strong cup of coffee and let it cool to room temperature. If using coffee liqueur, mix it into the cooled coffee.

Prepare Egg Yolk Mixture:

- In a heatproof bowl, whisk together egg yolks and granulated sugar. Place the bowl over a pot of simmering water (double boiler) and whisk continuously until the mixture thickens and becomes pale. Remove from heat and let it cool slightly.

Add Mascarpone:

● Add softened mascarpone cheese to the egg yolk mixture and whisk until smooth.

Whip Heavy Cream:

● In a separate bowl, whip the heavy cream with vanilla extract until stiff peaks form.

Fold in Whipped Cream:

● Gently fold the whipped cream into the mascarpone mixture until well combined. Be careful not to deflate the whipped cream.

Assemble Tiramisu:

● Dip ladyfinger cookies into the brewed coffee (and coffee liqueur mixture if using) and place them at the bottom of the serving glasses to create a layer.

Layer Mascarpone Mixture:

● Spoon a layer of the mascarpone mixture over the dipped ladyfingers.

Repeat Layers:

● Repeat the process to create a second layer of dipped ladyfingers followed by a layer of mascarpone mixture.

Chill:

● Cover the serving glasses with plastic wrap and refrigerate for at least 4 hours or overnight to allow the flavors to meld.

Dust with Cocoa Powder:

● Before serving, dust the top of each Tiramisu with cocoa powder.

Garnish (Optional):

● Garnish with chocolate shavings for an extra touch of elegance.

Serve and Enjoy:

● Share and enjoy this delightful Tiramisu for Two with your loved one.

Chocolate-Covered Pretzel Decorating

Create sweet and salty treats with a fun and interactive chocolate-covered pretzel decorating activity. Perfect for a date night or a creative family activity, this idea allows you to customize your pretzels with various toppings. Here's a simple guide to get you started:

Ingredients:

● Pretzel rods or pretzel twists

● Chocolate for melting (dark, milk, or white chocolate)

● Toppings:

> ● Chopped nuts (e.g., almonds, pecans)
>
> ● Sprinkles
>
> ● Shredded coconut
>
> ● Mini chocolate chips
>
> ● Crushed candy canes
>
> ● Edible glitter (optional)

Instructions:

Melt Chocolate:

> ● Melt the chocolate in a heatproof bowl. You can use a microwave or a double boiler. Stir the chocolate until smooth.

Dip Pretzels:

> ● Dip each pretzel rod or twist into the melted chocolate, covering it completely.

Allow Excess to Drip:

> ● Allow the excess chocolate to drip off the pretzel back into the bowl.

Place on Parchment Paper:

> ● Place the chocolate-covered pretzels on a parchment paper-lined tray.

Add Toppings:

> ● While the chocolate is still wet, sprinkle your choice of toppings onto the pretzels. Get creative and mix and match toppings for a variety of flavors and textures.

Set and Decorate:

- Allow the chocolate and toppings to set. You can speed up the process by placing the tray in the refrigerator for about 15-20 minutes.

Drizzle with More Chocolate (Optional):

- If you want to add an extra decorative touch, melt a different color or type of chocolate and drizzle it over the pretzels using a spoon or a piping bag.

Let Set Completely:

- Allow the drizzled chocolate to set completely before handling the pretzels.

Arrange and Serve:

- Once everything is set, arrange the chocolate-covered pretzels on a serving platter. They are now ready to be enjoyed!

Gift Idea (Optional):

- Package the decorated pretzels in clear cellophane bags and tie them with a ribbon for a delightful homemade gift.

Enjoy the Sweet and Salty Treats:

- Share and enjoy your customized chocolate-covered pretzels with friends, family, or your loved ones.

Tips for Setting the Perfect Valentine's Day Table

Creating a romantic and inviting atmosphere for your Valentine's Day celebration involves more than just a delicious meal. Here are some tips for setting the perfect Valentine's Day table:

Choose a Romantic Color Palette:

- Opt for a color scheme that exudes romance. Classic choices include shades of red, pink, white, and gold. Consider using elegant and muted tones for a sophisticated touch.

Use Elegant Tableware:

- Bring out your best dinnerware, flatware, and glassware. Consider using fine china or decorative plates for a special touch. Polished silverware and crystal glasses add a luxurious feel.

Create a Centerpiece:

- Craft a beautiful centerpiece that complements the theme. A bouquet of fresh flowers, especially roses, is a timeless choice. You can also use candles, lanterns, or fairy lights for a warm and intimate glow.

Personalized Place Settings:

- Add a personal touch by incorporating place cards or personalized name tags. Consider small tokens or love notes at each place setting to make it extra special.

Soft Lighting is Key:

- Choose soft and ambient lighting to create a cozy and intimate atmosphere. Candles or fairy lights on the table or around the room can enhance the romantic ambiance.

Use Fine Linens:

- Dress the table with high-quality tablecloths, napkins, and placemats. Opt for fabrics like satin or linen for an elegant touch. Consider using cloth napkins folded decoratively.

Incorporate Romantic Details:

- Integrate romantic details such as heart-shaped decor, delicate lace, or subtle Valentine's Day-themed elements. Avoid going overboard to maintain an elegant look.

Play Soft Background Music:

- Create a romantic ambiance with soft and soothing background music. Choose music that holds sentimental value or aligns with the overall mood.

Consider a Sweetheart Table:

- If space allows, set up a sweetheart table for just the two of you. This intimate arrangement allows for focused conversation and creates a more romantic setting.

Add Texture and Layers:

- Layering adds visual interest to the table. Use chargers, layered plates, and textured table runners to create depth. Consider incorporating textured elements like lace or satin for a luxurious feel.

Serve a Special Drink:

- Begin the evening with a special welcome drink. It could be champagne, a signature cocktail, or a non-alcoholic beverage. Use decorative glasses and garnishes for an extra touch.

Don't Forget Dessert:

- If dessert is part of your celebration, set up a dessert station with beautifully plated treats. Consider a dessert charcuterie board or a selection of sweet indulgences.

Fresh Scents:

- Consider adding a subtle fragrance to the table with scented candles or fresh flowers. Choose scents like rose, lavender, or vanilla for a romantic touch.

Keep it Intimate:

- Keep the table setting intimate by minimizing clutter. A clean and well-organized table enhances the overall dining experience.

Romantic Table Decor Ideas

Transform your dining space into a romantic haven with these enchanting table decor ideas for a special Valentine's Day celebration:

Candlelit Elegance:

- Create a dreamy atmosphere with an abundance of candles. Use candlesticks, votives, or tealights to cast a warm and romantic glow over the table.

Floral Romance:

- Arrange a beautiful bouquet of fresh flowers as a centerpiece. Roses are a classic choice, but you can also mix in other blooms like lilies, tulips, or peonies for variety.

Rose Petal Pathway:

- Scatter rose petals along the center of the table or create a romantic pathway leading to each seat. This simple touch adds a touch of luxury and romance.

Heartfelt Decor:

- Incorporate heart-shaped elements into the decor. This can include heart-shaped napkin rings, heart confetti, or heart-themed place cards.

Lace and Linens:

- Use lace or satin tablecloths, napkins, and placemats for an elegant and romantic feel. The luxurious textures add a touch of sophistication.

Gold and Red Accents:

- Combine the richness of gold with the passion of red. Gold-trimmed dinnerware, red napkins, and gold candle holders create a regal and romantic setting.

String Lights Magic:

- Hang string lights above the table for a magical ambiance. Choose warm white lights to create a cozy and intimate atmosphere.

Chic Charger Plates:

- Elevate the table setting with stylish charger plates. Opt for gold or silver chargers to add a touch of glamour.

Personalized Touch:

- Add a personalized touch with customized place cards or small love notes at each setting. This thoughtful detail enhances the intimate feel of the celebration.

Fairy Tale Lanterns:

- Incorporate lanterns with LED candles for a fairytale-inspired look. Choose lanterns in metallic tones for a touch of opulence.

Gilded Flatware:

- Consider using gilded or gold-toned flatware to bring a touch of luxury to the table setting. This subtle detail adds a romantic and regal vibe.

Vintage Romance:

- Create a vintage-inspired table with antique candle holders, vintage china, and lace doilies. The nostalgic charm adds a romantic touch.

Ribbon Accents:

● Tie silk or satin ribbons around napkins or chairs for an elegant and whimsical touch. Choose colors that complement your overall theme.

Sculptural Centerpiece:

● Choose a unique sculptural centerpiece that complements the romantic theme. This could be an artfully arranged collection of candles, a heart-shaped floral arrangement, or a decorative sculpture.

Crystal Elegance:

● Add crystal elements to the table, such as crystal glasses, vases, or candle holders. The sparkle and shine enhance the romantic ambiance.

Whimsical Balloons:

● Incorporate heart-shaped or metallic balloons for a whimsical touch. Tie them to the back of chairs or create a balloon bouquet as a centerpiece.

Draped Fabric:

● Use draped fabric as a table runner or to add a layer of softness to the table. Choose fabrics like tulle or chiffon for a romantic and ethereal effect.

Festive Confetti:

● Sprinkle heart-shaped confetti or metallic confetti on the table for a festive and celebratory vibe.

Fragrant Elements:

● Place scented candles or diffusers with romantic fragrances like rose, jasmine, or lavender to enhance the sensory experience.

Chic Wine Glasses:

● Opt for chic and sophisticated wine glasses. Consider goblets with gold rims or engraved details for an extra touch of elegance.

Choosing the Right Wine for Your Meal

Choosing the right wine for your meal involves considering the flavors, textures, and intensity of both the food and the wine. Here are some general guidelines to help you pair wine with different types of meals:

White Wines:

● Light and Crisp Whites (e.g., Sauvignon Blanc, Pinot Grigio):

- Ideal for light and fresh dishes such as salads, seafood, and dishes with citrus flavors.

- Medium to Full-bodied Whites (e.g., Chardonnay, Viognier):

- Pair well with creamy dishes, richer seafood, poultry, and dishes with buttery or nutty elements.

Red Wines:

- Light and Fruity Reds (e.g., Pinot Noir, Gamay):

- Complement dishes with earthy or herbal flavors, such as roasted chicken, pork, or mushroom-based dishes.

- Medium-bodied Reds (e.g., Merlot, Chianti):

- Versatile and can be paired with various dishes, including pasta, grilled meats, and tomato-based sauces.

- Bold Reds (e.g., Cabernet Sauvignon, Syrah):

- Suitable for hearty and flavorful dishes such as grilled steaks, lamb, and dishes with rich, savory sauces.

Rosé:

- Dry Rosé:

- A versatile choice that pairs well with light salads, seafood, and grilled vegetables. Also complements Mediterranean and spicy cuisines.

Sparkling Wines:

- Champagne, Prosecco, Cava:

- Classic pairings with appetizers, salty snacks, seafood, and dishes with creamy or buttery sauces. Also a great palate cleanser.

Dessert Wines:

- Sweet White Wines (e.g., Sauternes, Late Harvest Riesling):

- Perfect with desserts like fruit tarts, cheesecake, or dishes with sweet and savory elements.

- Port or Fortified Wines:

- Pair well with rich chocolate desserts, nuts, and strong cheeses.

Consider the Sauce:

- If your dish has a rich or savory sauce, consider the characteristics of the sauce when choosing the wine. For example, a creamy pasta sauce might pair well with a fuller-bodied white or a light red.

Balance Intensity:

> ● Match the intensity of the wine with the intensity of the food. Lighter dishes generally pair well with lighter wines, while heartier or spicier dishes can stand up to more robust wines.

Regional Pairings:

> ● Consider traditional pairings based on the cuisine's region. For example, Italian dishes often pair well with Italian wines, and French cuisine may be complemented by French wines.

Personal Preferences:

> ● Ultimately, personal preferences play a significant role. If you enjoy a certain wine with a particular dish, go with what you love.

Experiment and Explore:

> ● Don't be afraid to experiment and try different pairings. Wine and food pairing is subjective, and you may discover unique combinations that suit your taste.

Creating a Cozy Atmosphere

Creating a cozy atmosphere involves a combination of elements that engage the senses and promote a sense of warmth and comfort. Here are some tips to help you create a cozy and inviting ambiance:

Soft Lighting:

- Opt for soft and warm lighting rather than harsh overhead lights. Use table lamps, floor lamps, or string lights to create a gentle glow. Candles also add a cozy and romantic touch.

Warm Color Palette:

- Choose warm and earthy colors for your decor, such as soft neutrals, warm browns, and deep reds. These colors create a comfortable and inviting atmosphere.

Comfortable Textiles:

- Layer soft and plush textiles throughout your space. Add throw blankets, cushions, and soft area rugs to create a cozy and tactile environment.

Natural Elements:

- Bring in natural elements like wood, stone, or plants. Wooden furniture, stone accents, and indoor plants add a touch of nature and warmth to your space.

Comfortable Seating:

- Invest in comfortable and inviting seating. Whether it's a plush sofa, cozy armchairs, or floor cushions, ensure that your seating encourages relaxation.

Texture Variety:

- Mix and match textures to add depth to your decor. Incorporate textures like faux fur, knit, or velvet for a tactile and inviting feel.

Soft Music:

- Play soft and soothing music in the background. Choose genres like acoustic, jazz, or classical to create a calming atmosphere.

Scented Candles or Diffusers:

- Use scented candles or diffusers to introduce comforting scents. Fragrances like vanilla, lavender, or cinnamon can enhance the cozy ambiance.

Books and Reading Nooks:

- Create a cozy reading nook with a comfortable chair, soft lighting, and a collection of your favorite books. This provides a perfect retreat for relaxation.

Warm Beverages:

- Prepare warm beverages like tea, hot chocolate, or mulled wine. The aroma and warmth of these drinks contribute to the overall cozy atmosphere.

Soft Throws and Pillows:

- Drape soft throws over furniture and add an abundance of pillows. This not only enhances comfort but also adds visual warmth to the space.

Fireplace or Faux Fire Element:

- If you have a fireplace, light it up for a warm and inviting focal point. If not, consider using a faux fire element or candles to create the illusion of a fireplace.

Dimmers or Smart Lighting:

- Install dimmers on your lights or use smart lighting systems to adjust the brightness according to your mood. Lowering the lights enhances the cozy ambiance.

Personalized Decor:

- Decorate with personal items that hold sentimental value. Family photos, cherished mementos, and personal artwork contribute to a cozy and homey feel.

Layered Drapes:

- Use layered drapes or curtains to add a sense of warmth and privacy. Thick, insulating curtains can also help with temperature control.

Blanket Basket:

- Keep a basket of blankets or throws within reach. This encourages snuggling up and adds an extra layer of comfort.

Unplugged Time:

- Set aside time to unplug from electronic devices. Embrace quiet moments for reading, conversation, or simply enjoying the cozy atmosphere.

Floral Arrangements for the Perfect Ambiance

Enhance the ambiance of your space with beautiful floral arrangements that bring a touch of nature and elegance. Here are some ideas for creating the perfect floral arrangements:

Seasonal Blooms:

- Choose flowers that are in season to create a fresh and vibrant arrangement. Seasonal blooms not only look beautiful but also add a natural and authentic touch to your space.

Monochromatic Elegance:

- Create an elegant and cohesive look by sticking to a monochromatic color scheme. Choose flowers in shades of one color, such as all-white, for a timeless and sophisticated arrangement.

Wildflower Charm:

- Embrace the beauty of wildflowers for a charming and rustic arrangement. Mix different varieties of wildflowers for a relaxed and natural feel.

Minimalist Chic:

- Opt for a minimalist approach by selecting a single type of flower and arranging them in a simple vase. This creates a chic and understated look that is perfect for modern spaces.

Cascading Beauty:

- Create a romantic and cascading arrangement by arranging flowers with varying stem lengths. Let the blooms spill over the edges of the vase for a whimsical and captivating display.

Scented Delight:

- Choose fragrant flowers to add a delightful scent to your space. Flowers like roses, lilies, or lavender not only look beautiful but also contribute to a pleasant aroma.

Tall and Dramatic:

- Opt for tall flowers or branches to create a dramatic and eye-catching arrangement. Tall floral centerpieces can be a stunning focal point for special occasions.

Vintage Charm:

- Arrange flowers in vintage or antique containers for a touch of nostalgia. Consider using old teacups, mason jars, or vintage vases to add character to your floral display.

Tropical Paradise:

- Create a tropical vibe with exotic flowers and greenery. Orchids, birds of paradise, and tropical foliage can bring a touch of paradise to your space.

Dried Florals:

- Explore the beauty of dried florals for a long-lasting arrangement. Dried flowers in muted tones add a rustic and vintage charm to your decor.

Sunflowers for Cheerfulness:

- Use sunflowers for a burst of cheerful color. Their bright yellow petals bring a sense of happiness and warmth to any room.

Herb Infusion:

- Integrate fragrant herbs like lavender, rosemary, or mint into your floral arrangement. The combination of flowers and herbs creates a delightful sensory experience.

Floating Blooms:

- Float delicate blooms in a shallow bowl or vase filled with water. This ethereal arrangement adds a serene vibe to your space.

Petal Pathway:

- Scatter petals along a pathway or surface for a romantic and whimsical touch. This works well for special occasions or as a decorative element in the home.

All-White Elegance:

- Create an atmosphere of sophistication and purity with an all-white floral arrangement. White flowers symbolize purity and elegance and can be perfect for formal settings.

Personalized Place Cards for a Special Touch

Add a thoughtful and personal touch to your dining experience by creating personalized place cards for your guests. Here are creative ideas to make each place setting unique:

Calligraphy Name Cards:

- Hire a calligrapher or practice your calligraphy skills to create elegant name cards. Use high-quality paper or small cardstock for a sophisticated touch.

Leafy Greenery Tags:

- Attach small sprigs of greenery, such as eucalyptus or rosemary, to each place card. Tie them with twine or ribbon for a fresh and natural look.

Mini Photo Frames:

 • Place mini photo frames at each setting with a photo of each guest. This adds a personal and nostalgic touch, and guests can take the frames home as keepsakes.

Seating Stones:

 • Use smooth stones or river rocks as place cards. Write each guest's name on a stone using a metallic pen or paint for a natural and rustic feel.

Edible Place Cards:

 • Incorporate edible elements into your place cards. Write names on cookies, macarons, or chocolate truffles for a sweet and delightful surprise.

Vintage Key Tags:

 • Attach vintage-style key tags with each guest's name written or printed on them. This works especially well for weddings or events with a romantic theme.

Felt Leaf Cutouts:

 • Cut out leaf shapes from colorful felt and write or embroider each guest's name. These charming leaf place cards bring a touch of autumnal warmth to the table.

Origami Creations:

 • Fold small origami shapes, such as cranes or hearts, and write names on them. Origami place cards add an artistic and intricate touch.

Wine Cork Place Card Holders:

 • Slice a thin section off the end of the wine corks and attach a card with each guest's name. This rustic and eco-friendly option is perfect for wine-themed events.

Dip-Dyed Watercolor Cards:

 • Create a beautiful ombre effect by dip-dyeing place cards in watercolor. Write names with a contrasting color for a modern and artistic look.

Succulent Name Tags:

 • Attach small potted succulents to each place card. Guests can take these home as party favors, extending the memory beyond the event.

Ribbon Wrapped Cards:

- Wrap place cards with colorful ribbons, securing them with a bow. This adds a touch of elegance and is a great way to incorporate your event's color scheme.

Chalkboard Tags:

- Use small chalkboard tags or pieces of chalkboard paper as place cards. Guests can write personal messages or doodles on them throughout the event.

Sprinkle of Confetti:

- Sprinkle a few confetti pieces around each place card. This adds a festive and celebratory element to the table setting.

Personalized Coasters:

- Use personalized coasters with each guest's name. This functional and decorative element also protects your table from drink condensation.

Quirky and Fun Tags:

- Get creative with tags that reflect the personality of each guest. Consider using funny quotes, inside jokes, or personalized compliments.

Stamped Wooden Discs:

- Stamp each guest's name onto small wooden discs. These can be reused for other events or as home decor.

Luggage Tag Place Cards:

- Attach small luggage tags to each place setting. This is a great idea for travel-themed events and provides a unique and functional keepsake.

Conclusion

As you prepare for your Valentine's Day celebration, the key is to create an atmosphere that is not only romantic but also reflects your personal style and thoughtful touches. From a warm welcome in the introduction to the culinary delights of the main courses and sweet endings, and the perfect drinks for toasting, each element contributes to a memorable experience.

The table settings, floral arrangements, and personalized place cards add a touch of elegance and individuality to your celebration. Incorporating cozy elements and creating a welcoming ambiance enhances the overall experience, making it a celebration to remember.

Whether you're planning a romantic dinner for two or a gathering with loved ones, the recipes, decor ideas, and tips provided are designed to help you craft a Valentine's Day celebration filled with love, joy, and delightful moments.

Glossary

Aphrodisiac:

- Foods or substances believed to enhance romantic or sexual desire.

Bisque:

- A smooth and creamy soup, often made from shellfish, vegetables, or fruits.

Bruschetta:

- Grilled or toasted bread rubbed with garlic and topped with various ingredients like tomatoes, basil, and olive oil.

Crostini:

- Small slices of toasted or grilled bread, typically topped with various spreads or toppings.

Gazpacho:

- A cold Spanish soup made from tomatoes, peppers, onions, cucumbers, and other vegetables.

Lobster Bisque:

- A rich and creamy soup made with lobster broth and often finished with cream.

Marsala:

- A type of wine, often used in cooking, particularly in the preparation of Chicken Marsala.

Risotto:

- An Italian dish made with arborio rice, cooked slowly with broth until creamy.

Caprese:

- A salad made with fresh tomatoes, mozzarella cheese, basil, and olive oil.

Fondue:

- A dish in which small pieces of food are dipped into a hot, melted mixture, typically of cheese or chocolate.

Martini:

- A cocktail made with gin or vodka and vermouth typically garnished with an olive or a twist of lemon.

Bellini:

- A cocktail made with Prosecco and peach puree or nectar.

Sorbet:

- A frozen dessert made from sweetened water with flavorings, often fruit juice.

Molten Lava Cake:

- A dessert with a gooey, liquid center, usually made with chocolate.

Charcuterie Board:

- A platter of assorted cured meats, cheeses, fruits, and condiments.

Champagne Cream Sauce:

- A sauce made with champagne or sparkling wine, often used to accompany seafood or poultry.

Red Wine Reduction:

- A sauce made by simmering red wine to concentrate its flavors, often used with beef or lamb.

Truffle Mashed Potatoes:

- Mashed potatoes infused with truffle oil or truffle butter for a rich and earthy flavor.

Cinnamon French Toast Sticks:

- Slices of bread coated in a mixture of eggs, milk, and cinnamon, then pan-fried until golden brown.

Chia Pudding:

- A pudding made by soaking chia seeds in liquid is often served as a healthy breakfast or dessert.

Tiramisu:

- An Italian dessert made with layers of coffee-soaked ladyfingers and mascarpone cheese.

Chocolate-Covered Pretzels:

- Pretzels coated in chocolate and often topped with various sweet or salty toppings.

Place Cards:

- Small cards or tags with the names of guests are used to indicate assigned seating at a table.

String Lights:

- Decorative lights are often used to create a warm and cozy ambiance.

Calligraphy:

- Artistic handwriting is often used for creating elegant and decorative lettering.

Monochromatic:

- Consisting of or using only one color.

Confetti:

- Small pieces of colored paper or other materials are thrown as a celebration or decoration.

Ombre:

- A gradual blending of one color to another, often creating a shaded or gradient effect.

Eco-Friendly:

- Environmentally friendly or sustainable, often referring to products or practices that have minimal impact on the environment.

Origami:

- The Japanese art of paper folding to create intricate and decorative shapes.

Disclaimer:

The information provided in this cookbook is for general informational purposes only and is not intended as professional advice. The recipes, tips, and suggestions contained herein are based on personal experiences and preferences. Before attempting any recipe or decor idea, readers should consider their individual dietary preferences, restrictions, and health conditions.

While every effort has been made to ensure the accuracy and completeness of the information in this cookbook, the author and publisher make no representations or warranties of any kind, express or implied, about the completeness, accuracy, reliability, suitability, or availability of the information, recipes, or related graphics. Any reliance placed on such information is strictly at the reader's own risk.

The recipes contained in this cookbook may involve the use of kitchen appliances, utensils, and cooking techniques. Readers should exercise caution and adhere to safety guidelines when handling kitchen equipment and cooking ingredients. The author and publisher are not responsible for any injury, harm, or adverse effects resulting from the use of information provided in this cookbook.

The inclusion of specific brands, products, or external links does not imply endorsement or sponsorship. Readers are encouraged to use their discretion and conduct their own research when considering external recommendations.

Don't miss out!

Visit the website below and you can sign up to receive emails whenever David Meyer publishes a new book. There's no charge and no obligation.

https://books2read.com/r/B-A-MITZ-BNTUC

BOOKS 2 READ

Connecting independent readers to independent writers.

Also by David Meyer

Love in the Kitchen: A Valentine's Day Cookbook

www.ingramcontent.com/pod-product-compliance
Lightning Source LLC
Chambersburg PA
CBHW081149130726
47996CB00009B/3052